ABE

&

FIDO

LINCOLN'S LOVE *of* ANIMALS

and the

TOUCHING STORY

OF HIS

FAVORITE

CANINE

COMPANION

MATTHEW ALGEO

Copyright © 2015 by Matthew Algeo
All rights reserved
Published by Chicago Review Press, Incorporated
814 North Franklin Street
Chicago, Illinois 60610
ISBN 978-1-55652-222-2

Library of Congress Cataloging-in-Publication Data
Algeo, Matthew.
  Abe & Fido : Lincoln's love of animals and the touching story of his
favorite canine companion / Matthew Algeo.
     pages cm
  Includes bibliographical references and index.
  ISBN 978-1-55652-222-2
  1. Lincoln, Abraham, 1809–1865. 2. Fido (Dog), 1855–1866. 3.
Presidents' pets—United States—History—19th century. 4. Dogs—
United States—Biography. 5. Human-animal relationships—United
States—History—19th century. I. Title. II. Title: Abe and Fido.
  E457.25.A44 2015
  973.7092—dc23
                              2014047591

Interior design: Jonathan Hahn

Printed in the United States of America
5 4 3 2 1

TO FRANK AND GIGI

Near this Spot
are deposited the Remains of one
who possessed Beauty without Vanity,
Strength without Insolence,
Courage without Ferocity,
and all the virtues of Man without his Vices.

—**LORD BYRON**, *Epitaph to a Dog*

CONTENTS

PREFACE

The interval between Abraham Lincoln's election in November 1860 and his inauguration the following March brought, in his words, "multifarious demands upon my time and attention." This was to be expected; after all, the country was falling apart. In late December, South Carolina seceded, and by the end of January 1861 five more states would follow the Palmetto State out of the Union. Meanwhile, Lincoln's efforts to assemble a cabinet—his famous "team of rivals"— were foundering; he found it nearly impossible to placate the innumerable competing political and sectional factions, leaving him to grumble that "really great men were scarcer than they used to be."

Lincoln spent much of this time in his hometown of Springfield, Illinois, holed up in a small room in the dry goods store owned by his brother-in-law, Clark M. Smith. The room was furnished with nothing but a simple desk and a chair. Here Lincoln struggled to compose his inaugural address while doing his best to avoid the hordes of office seekers who had descended on Springfield like a plague of winter locusts, beseeching the president-elect for everything from lowly postmasterships to plum diplomatic posts.

Yet, of all the weighty tasks facing Lincoln as he prepared to take the reins of a nation tearing itself apart, perhaps none weighed more heavily on his mind, none did he dread more, than delivering the heartbreaking news to his two youngest boys, Willie and Tad, that the family's beloved dog Fido would not be accompanying them to Washington. Lincoln felt the long rail journey would be too stressful for the skittish dog; it would be better to leave him behind with friends in Springfield.

When Lincoln finally broke the news to the boys, they were devastated. Surely there were tears. The boys—in January 1861 Willie was ten and Tad seven—protested that they could care for the dog on the trip and in Washington too. Lincoln was an indulgent parent—he believed children should be "free, happy, and unrestrained by parental tyranny"—but in this instance he stood firm: Fido must stay. It must've taken all his considerable powers of statesmanship to convince the boys of the soundness of his decision. After all, they had practically grown up with the friendly yellow mutt. Eventually, reluctantly, the boys agreed.

That Abraham Lincoln put the welfare of Fido above his children's tearful pleadings is indicative of just how much he cared for the dog—and for all animals.

Animals had always played a central role in Abraham Lincoln's life. As a young man, the kindness he showed them was practically unique on the frontier. At a time when pulling the heads off live geese was considered a perfectly reasonable way to pass the time, Lincoln preached that all living creatures were deserving of tender mercy—even ants. He thought nothing of rescuing animals in distress: a pig stuck in mud, orphaned kittens, even hatchlings separated from their mother. He owned pets throughout his life—"yaller dogs" like Fido were a particular favorite—and as president he often found solace in the company of animals. His White House was a veritable menagerie, with a dog, cats, rabbits, goats, and ponies.

Yet the role that animals played in Lincoln's life has been largely overlooked by his biographers, who often relegate his encounters with animals to mawkish sidebars. Maybe that's not surprising, considering the momentousness of his life's accomplishments. Still, it is an aspect of Lincoln's personality that demands further inspection; indeed, it may be the one area of his life not fully examined.

Through the president's relationship with his beloved Fido, this book will tell the larger story of Abraham Lincoln's attitude toward animals in general, an attitude that animated his life and even his presidency. As the Lincoln biographer Michael Burlingame has written, "Lincoln's outrage at the mistreatment of animals foreshadowed his indignation at the cruelties of slavery."

By his association with Lincoln, Fido became the most famous dog in America. His image was reproduced on a *carte de visite*, a kind of nineteenth-century trading card, which became a popular souvenir after Lincoln's death. Fido's name was so famous that it practically became a synonym for the family dog—and still is.

I hope this book will shed at least a glimmer of new light on Abraham Lincoln, America's most analyzed president.

Mostly, though, this tale is the simple story of a man and his dog. Both were famous, beloved, and, as we shall see, ultimately tragic figures.

If not for Lincoln, we never would have heard of a yellow mutt named Fido. And as anyone who has over owned a pet can attest, without Fido, Lincoln's life would have been a little less complete.

1

1855

HAD HE DIED IN 1855, Abraham Lincoln's life would have been judged a great success, the epitome of what later generations would call the American Dream. Born into poverty in a Kentucky log cabin on February 12, 1809, he'd practically taught himself to read and write. As a young man he moved to Illinois, where he studied law (again, independently), and with his friend William Herndon, built a thriving law practice in the state capital, Springfield. He'd served four terms in the Illinois legislature and one in the US House of Representatives. And he'd married well: Mary Todd, whom he'd wed in 1842, came from a distinguished (and, certainly by Lincoln's standards, wealthy) Kentucky family. He and Mary had three children: Robert, Willie, and Tad. (Their second son, Edward, had died just short of his fourth birthday in 1850.)

Abraham Lincoln had earned universal respect among those who knew him well. He was one of Springfield's most beloved and trusted citizens, renowned for his fairness as well as his good humor.

Yet in 1855 Lincoln considered himself a failure. At times he might even have wished he were dead. Early that

year, shortly before his forty-sixth birthday, he'd narrowly
lost a bid for a seat in the US Senate. At the time, senators
were chosen by state legislatures. In Illinois the legislature
comprised seventy-five representatives and twenty-five senators, so fifty-one votes were needed to win a seat. On the
first ballot, Lincoln, running as the Whig candidate, received
forty-five. But his vote total diminished with each succeed-
ing ballot, and the seat eventually went to Lyman Trumbull, an antislavery Democrat who would go on to serve
three terms in the Senate. (Trumbull cowrote the Thirteenth
Amendment, which abolished slavery.)

Publicly, Lincoln was stoic. He congratulated Trumbull
and even attended his victory party, where he admitted he
was disappointed, though "not *too* disappointed to congrat-
ulate my friend Trumbull." (Later Lincoln would hail Trumbull "for his rigid honesty, his high-toned independence, &
his unswerving devotion to principle.")

Privately, however, Lincoln was devastated, and the loss
plunged him into a deep depression. According to his law
partner, William Herndon, Lincoln "thirsted for public
notice and hungered—longed for approbation and when
he did not get that notice or that approbation—and was not
thoroughly appreciated . . . he writhed under it."

Elihu B. Washburne, a congressman from Illinois (and
future US secretary of state) who was one of Lincoln's staunch-
est supporters, later wrote that "no event in Mr. Lincoln's
entire political career . . . brought to him so much disap-
pointment and chagrin" as his defeat in the 1855 Senate race.

"I never saw him so dejected," another supporter, Joseph
Gillespie, remembered. "He said the fates seemed to be

against him and he thought he would never strive for office again."

Lincoln had devoted so much time and energy to the Senate race that he had neglected his law practice, and immediately afterward he was forced to "pick up [his] lost crumbs." That summer he jumped at the chance to join a team of lawyers representing John H. Manny, the inventor of a mechanical reaper, who was being sued by Cyrus Hall McCormick for patent infringement.

Manny's legal team was headed by a Philadelphia lawyer named George Harding. Since he expected the case to be tried in a federal court in Chicago, Harding thought it would be a good idea to have an Illinois lawyer on the team, though, he noted condescendingly, "we were not likely to find a lawyer there who would be of real assistance in arguing such a case." Harding was referred to Lincoln and offered him a $400 retainer—roughly $10,000 in today's money—which Lincoln gladly accepted.

Unexpectedly, the court moved the case to Cincinnati. When Lincoln showed up for the trial, he found his presence neither expected nor welcomed. Harding, who had never seen Lincoln in person before, described him as "a tall, rawly boned, ungainly backwoodsman, with coarse, ill-fitting clothing." Another lawyer on Manny's team, the brilliant Edwin M. Stanton, was equally unimpressed with the poorly clad Illinoisan, whom he dismissed as "a low-down country lawyer."

"Why did you bring that d——d long armed Ape here," Stanton asked Harding. "He does not know any thing and can do you no good." Lincoln was relegated to the role of spectator during the weeklong trial. And even though he stayed in the same hotel as the other lawyers, none of them would deign to speak with him. He was completely ostracized. Harding later admitted that neither he nor Stanton "ever conferred with him, ever had him at our table or sat with him, or asked him to our room, or walked to or from the court with him, or, in fact, had any intercourse with him." (Incidentally, their client won the case.)

It was a humiliating experience for Lincoln. When he returned to Springfield, he confided to his law partner, William Herndon, that he had been "roughly handled" in Cincinnati. (Still, never one to hold a grudge, Lincoln would make Edwin Stanton his secretary of war in 1862. For his part Stanton would later admit, "What a mistake I made about that man when I met him in Cincinnati.")

His mistreatment at the hands of Manny's lawyers, coupled with his failed bid to win the Senate seat earlier that year, only deepened Lincoln's depression. In fact, he'd been acting erratically for some time. His friend and fellow lawyer Henry Clay Whitney, who sometimes shared a room with Lincoln when the two men traveled the judicial circuit, said Lincoln suffered from nightmares. One night Whitney awoke to find his roommate "sitting up in his bed . . . talking the wildest and most incoherent nonsense all to himself." Whitney said a "stranger to Lincoln would have supposed he had suddenly gone insane."

Throughout his life, Lincoln was tortured by self-doubt, haunted by what he called "the hypo," short for *hypochondriasis*, a common term back then for depression and intense anxiety. Always cognizant of his own mortality, he measured his achievements against his ambitions and felt he'd come up short. He dwelled on goals unmet, dreams unfulfilled. Henry Clay Whitney said he "had never seen him so melancholy" as he was in 1855.

His home on the corner of Eighth and Jackson in Springfield offered little respite from his melancholia. His wife, Mary, was moody and cantankerous, prone to erratic behavior, with a penchant for spending more money than her husband earned from his law practice. Their children—twelve-year-old Bob, four-year-old Willie, and two-year-old Tad, all of whom Lincoln adored—were a handful, especially the youngest two, who conspired in all manner of mischief. Tad, who was born with a cleft palate and suffered from a speech impediment, was given to fits of frustrated rage. Much of the burden of raising the boys fell on Lincoln, as Mary, according to her cousin Elizabeth Todd Grimsley, was "always over-anxious."

Understandably, the light brown house at Eighth and Jackson was not always a happy place for Lincoln. Friends often noted that he seemed to prefer spending time away from his home, either riding the circuit on one of his trusty horses to litigate cases in distant locales, or just working long hours in his law office on the town square. David Davis, the judge who presided over the courts on Lincoln's circuit, remembered that Lincoln had a "strange disinclination to go home" and "was not domestically happy."

Something else was haunting Lincoln in 1855, looming over him and the rest of the country like a specter: slavery. It was the era's defining moral and political question, and Lincoln spent much time brooding over it. He had always

The Lincoln home in 1861. COURTESY OF LIBRARY OF CONGRESS

found slavery reprehensible, but the passage of the Kansas-Nebraska Act the year before was forcing him (and the nation) to confront the issue once and for all. The act, sponsored by Stephen A. Douglas, a Democratic senator from Illinois and Lincoln's fiercest political rival, allowed each territory to decide for itself whether slavery would be permitted within its borders before applying for statehood. That decision would be made by a territorial legislature elected by the territory's (white male) residents. Supporters called this "popular sovereignty" and "the sacred right of self-government." Opponents called it a sham.

To Lincoln the Kansas-Nebraska Act was a transparent attempt to circumvent the Missouri Compromise of 1820, which had effectively confined slavery to the South. Lincoln believed that the Constitution prohibited Congress from abolishing slavery in the states where it already existed, but he adamantly opposed its expansion beyond the borders of those states. This put him at odds with one of his oldest friends, Joshua Speed, whom Lincoln had met the day he moved to Springfield in 1837. When the twenty-eight-year-old Lincoln walked into Speed's general store and asked him how much a new mattress, sheets, and a pillow would cost, Speed said seventeen dollars. Lincoln said he didn't have that much money, so Speed made him a generous offer: "I have a large room with a double-bed upstairs, which you are very welcome to share with me."

"Where is your room?" Lincoln asked.

Speed pointed to the staircase.

Lincoln carried his saddlebags up the stairs, came back down, and announced: "Well, Speed, I am moved."

The two young men would share a bed for the next three years, a common arrangement at the time, though some have speculated that their relationship was not strictly platonic. Carl Sandburg, whose Pulitzer Prize–winning biography of Lincoln is as verbose as it is unreliable, described the relationship as "a streak of lavender and spots soft as May violets" in the life of the future president.

Whatever its nature, the relationship endured; Lincoln and Speed would remain lifelong friends, and in their correspondence Lincoln revealed as much about his inner feelings as he ever would. By 1855, Speed had moved back to his native Kentucky, where he oversaw his family's plantation, which was tended by a number of slaves. In a long, heartfelt letter to Speed dated August 24, 1855, Lincoln revealed much about his thinking on slavery at the time and, with uncanny empathy, his understanding of how the other side thought as well:

Dear Speed:

You know what a poor correspondent I am. Ever
since I received your very agreeable letter of the
22nd. of May I have been intending to write you
in answer to it. You suggest that in political action
now, you and I would differ. I suppose we would;
not quite as much, however, as you may think.
You know I dislike slavery; and you fully admit the
abstract wrong of it. So far there is no cause of difference. But you say that sooner than yield your legal
right to the slave—especially at the bidding of those
who are not themselves interested, you would see
the Union dissolved. I am not aware that *any one* is
bidding you to yield that right; very certainly *I* am
not. I leave that matter entirely to yourself. I also
acknowledge *your* rights and *my* obligations, under
the constitution, in regard to your slaves. I confess
I hate to see the poor creatures hunted down, and
caught, and carried back to their stripes, and unre-
warded toils; but I bite my lip and keep quiet. In
1841 you and I had together a tedious low-water
trip, on a Steam Boat from Louisville to St. Louis.
You may remember, as I well do, that from Louisville
to the mouth of the Ohio, there were, on board,
ten or a dozen slaves, shackled together with irons.
That sight was a continued torment to me; and I
see something like it every time I touch the Ohio,
or any other slave-border. It is hardly fair for you to
assume, that I have no interest in a thing which has,
and continually exercises, the power of making me

miserable. You ought rather to appreciate how much the great body of the Northern people do crucify their feelings, in order to maintain their loyalty to the Constitution and the Union.

I do oppose the extension of slavery, because my judgment and feelings so prompt me; and I am under no obligation to the contrary. If for this you and I must differ, differ we must. . . .

You say if Kansas fairly votes herself a free state, as a Christian you will rather rejoice at it. All decent slaveholders *talk* that way; and I do not doubt their candor. But they never *vote* that way. Although in a private letter, or conversation, you will express your preference that Kansas shall be free, you would vote for no man for Congress who would say the same thing publicly. No such man could be elected from any district in a slave-state. . . .

Mary will probably pass a day to two in Louisville in October. My kindest regards to Mrs. Speed. On the leading subject of this letter, I have more of her sympathy that I have of yours.

And yet let [me] say I am Your friend forever
A. Lincoln

That same month, Lincoln wrote a letter to another Kentuckian, George Robertson, an eminent attorney who, during the debates over the Missouri Compromise thirty-five years earlier, had predicted "the peaceable elimination of slavery." Lincoln adamantly disagreed. He told Robertson that there was "no peaceful extinction of slavery in prospect for us." In his darkened mind, a civil war seemed inevitable.

"The Autocrat of all the Russias will resign his crown," he wrote in his letter to Robertson, "and proclaim his subjects free republicans sooner than will our American masters voluntarily give up their slaves."

In 1855 Abraham Lincoln found himself in a very dark place, facing an existential crisis. He had withdrawn from politics. He was reexamining his life. He was depressed by his own station, his perceived shortcomings, and the seemingly imminent dissolution of his beloved country. Biographer Michael Burlingame has described this period in Lincoln's life as his "midlife crisis."

So sometime that year, he got himself a dog: a yellow, long-eared mutt with a short bushy tail.

He named him Fido.

How Fido came to be part of the Lincoln family we do not know. He was probably a puppy at the time. We can imagine Lincoln walking home from work one evening and encountering an adorable stray: Lincoln, tall and lean in his stovepipe hat, bends his long frame to gently stroke the dog's mottled coat, and the pup follows him home. It's also possible that Willie or Tad found the dog and brought him home. Perhaps, as is often the case, it was the dog who adopted the family and not the other way around. One thing is certain: Lincoln did not buy the dog. While certain purebred dogs were bought and sold at the time, a mutt like Fido was so common as to be considered worthless.

Nor do we know precisely when Fido became part of the Lincoln family, but on this question a tantalizing clue lies buried in the dusty records of Diller's, a Springfield drugstore that went out of business during the Second World War. Jonathan Diller founded the business on the town square in 1839, and ten years later his cousin Roland Diller took it over. Roland Diller and his partner Charles Corneau would operate the pharmacy at various locations for the next sixty years, until 1899, when Roland's son Isaac took it over. Two years after that, in 1901, Isaac sold the business to go into real estate and insurance. Subsequent owners would run the pharmacy until 1945, when it finally closed for good after 106 years.

In the 1850s Diller's was much more than a drugstore. It was a local institution. Located near the state capitol, it was a kind of political clubhouse, where Springfield's business and political leaders gathered to discuss the issues of the day, great and small. As a prominent local attorney and some-time politician, Abraham Lincoln was naturally part of this coterie, and he and Roland Diller came to be good friends, despite the fact that Lincoln had once criticized Roland's cousin Jonathan, a Democrat, for being "an active partizan" when he served as the town's postmaster.

Diller's also sold candies, so the store was a popular hangout for local children as well, especially after a soda fountain was installed. In a 1900 letter to Roland Diller, Lincoln's eldest son, Robert, wrote, "It is far beyond my memory when I began to think Corneau & Diller's was a good place to go to, and I have no doubt all the boys of Springfield have been thinking so since I ceased to be a boy."

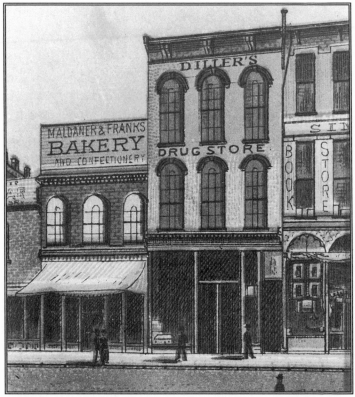

Diller's drugstore, a popular Springfield hangout, as it appeared around 1860. THE MESERVE-KUNHARDT FOUNDATION

It was among the mortars and pestles at Diller's that Abraham Lincoln debated issues as momentous as slavery and as mundane as public sewers. He also filled orders for various medicines and toiletries at Diller's and kept an account there that he paid off annually.

Roland Diller was a relatively minor character in Lincoln's life, but he bequeathed history a unique perspective on his friend and faithful customer, for despite several relocations and a devastating fire in 1858, some of the drugstore's records have, amazingly, survived: three daybooks, three ledgers, and a blotter, some of which contain notations pertaining to purchases Lincoln made between 1849 and 1861. These mundane records shed light on the ordinary, everyday lives of Lincoln and his family. They report, for example, that the man who would become one of our greatest presidents stopped by Diller's to pick up a bottle of cologne for fifty cents on Tuesday, May 27, 1851. Many of the purchases (such as that cologne) were probably intended for Mary. Mary likely used regular purchases of "essence of coffee"— actually a concoction of dried molasses that was mixed with coffee—to treat her migraines. Mary was also the consumer of Wright's Indian Vegetable Pills, a patent medicine that promised to cure "sick headaches, hysterics, weak nerves, low spirits, female complaints, and stomach and lung disorders." For his children Lincoln purchased numerous remedies for respiratory ailments: hive syrup (for cough and croup), sweet oil (a chest rub), and Wistar's Balsam of Wild Cherry (a patent medicine for consumption, asthma, and bronchitis). And although he was a teetotaler, Lincoln also purchased several pints of brandy at Diller's, though, as the Lincoln historian James T. Hickey pointed out, "brandy, during this period, was extensively used for medicinal purposes, as well as canning, pickling, and cooking."

Concerning Fido, one entry from 1855 is of special interest:

June 29, Bottle Vermifuge, .25

Vermifuge is a drug that expels worms in animals.

At the time, drugstores like Diller's dispensed medicines for animals as well as humans. Pharmacists were a community's de facto small-animal veterinarians. The first private veterinary schools had opened in large eastern cities by the 1850s, but these schools trained vets to care for horses and livestock. The common dog—a cur—was beneath their interest or expertise. So it was often left to pharmacists to diagnose ailments in household pets, prescribing remedies for everything from fleas to worms, the latter of which, it seems, had invaded poor Fido. Judging by this entry in Diller's ledgers, it is fair to assume that Fido had become part of the Lincoln family by the end of June 1855.

Lincoln was smitten by this bedraggled ball of yellow fur. He'd always had a soft spot for what, in his country accent, he called "yaller dogs." He'd owned one named Honey when he was a boy in Kentucky, and another, named Joe, when he was a young man in Indiana.

Lincoln's two youngest sons, Willie and Tad, likewise fell in love with Fido. Like their father, the two boys adored animals of all kinds. Tad, the youngest, was especially fond of them. "He was one of those children whom animals instinctively love," wrote Ruth Painter Randall in *Lincoln's Sons*. "Though he gave his pets strenuous treatment at times, they recognized his affection for them and his fundamental kindness."

Not everyone in the Lincoln home was enamored of its newest member, however. Mary Lincoln was terrified of dogs, even adorable puppies. Abe was extremely protective of his wife, and in their turbulent marriage he rarely failed to acquiesce to her demands, so it's noteworthy that he insisted on keeping the dog. That he did so is indicative of his feelings for Fido.

The eldest Lincoln son, twelve-year-old Bob, who took after his mother in many respects, wasn't much of a dog lover

Mary Lincoln in 1846 or 1847. A fear of dogs was one of her many phobias. COURTESY OF LIBRARY OF CONGRESS

either. His fear of dogs, however, was hardly irrational. It was rooted in a terrifying episode during his childhood.

WHEN BOB WAS A SMALL BOY, a dog bit him. The dog may have belonged to the Lincoln family. It may have been a stray. In any event, Mary was terrified, as there was no way to know if the dog was mad—that is, rabid. Always prone to fear the worst, Mary became convinced young Bob had contracted rabies, a virus carried in an infected animal's saliva.

Mary's fear was not wholly unjustified. Before Louis Pasteur and Émile Roux developed the first rabies vaccine in 1885, the disease was uniformly fatal. At the time, a popular treatment in such cases was a folk remedy that involved the use of a "mad stone." The "stone" was actually a calculus—basically a solidified hairball found in the organs of ruminants, animals that chew their cud. (The most effective mad stones were said to come from white deer.) Practitioners believed that, when applied to the wound, the mad stone would pull out the poison. Afterward, the stone was soaked in milk or water. If it leached out a greenish-yellow color—which was likely, considering it was a hairball, after all—this meant the poison had been successfully extracted. Problem was, mad stones were hard to come by—by tradition, they could not be bought or sold, and most were kept in families, handed down for generations like precious gems.

So, to treat Bob, Abe took him all the way to Terre Haute, Indiana, about 140 miles from Springfield, where a woman famous for her mad stone lived. It was a long and arduous trip over rough roads, but apparently the treatment was a success. When Bob returned to Springfield with his father, he was in perfect health.

FIDO MAY HAVE BEEN THE TOP DOG at the house on Eighth and Jackson, but he was not the Lincoln family's only pet. Lincoln seems to have had an open-door policy when it came to animals. Law partner Herndon once wrote (rather snidely) that if the Lincoln children "wanted a dog-cat-rat or the Devil it was all right and well treated—housed—petted—fed—fondled &c &c."

Cats were especially dear to Lincoln. He was neither strictly a dog person nor a cat person; he was that rare sort who loves both equally. There are many issues on which Abraham Lincoln took a firm, uncompromising stand; however, concerning the superiority of dogs or cats, the Great Emancipator was uncharacteristically noncommittal. He never went long without a pet dog, but cats, according to Mary, were his "hobby," and they seemed to have passed through the Lincoln home with regularity.

Mariah Vance, the Lincolns' African American housekeeper during the 1850s, recalled that the family had cats of all kinds: "little baby kittens . . . their mammy cats, an' big toms." With big toms and mammy cats about, it seems the Lincolns gave little thought to their pets' reproductive proclivities. This was not at all unusual at the time.

Vance remembered that Mary Lincoln didn't like having the cats in the house, so they lived mostly in the small barn behind the Lincoln home.

"With him a favorite way of forgetting his worries was to get down on the floor to pet and play with the cat," wrote Ruth Painter Randall, "stroking her under the chin and back of the ears, and talking to her in low caressing tones. He enjoyed, as all cat lovers do, the purring and little cat sounds that showed how she appreciated his gentle attentions."

Even birds did not escape his affection. Joshua Speed recalled a time when he was riding back to Springfield with Lincoln and several other attorneys, returning from a court session in another county seat. Lincoln and John J. Hardin were riding at the back of the pack, Speed recalled for the 1886 edition of a book called *The Every-Day Life of Abraham Lincoln.*

> "We had passed through a thicket of wild plum and crab-apple trees," says Mr. Speed, "and stopped to water our horses. Hardin came up alone. 'Where is Lincoln?' we inquired. 'Oh,' replied he, 'when I saw him last he had caught two young birds which the wind had blown out of their nest, and he was hunting the nest to put them back.' In a short time Lincoln came up, having found the nest and placed the young birds in it. The party laughed at him; but he said, 'I could not have slept if I had not restored those little birds to their mother.'"

Lincoln likewise loved horses. In 1889 there was roughly one horse for every five people in the United States. (Today there is one for every thirty-two people.) Not everyone owned a horse in the nineteenth century, but everyone depended on horses, which were the engines that drove the economy, and practically everyone was comfortable around the animals. Even if you didn't own a horse, you probably knew how to ride one. At the very least, you knew how to tie one to a post using a quick-release knot like the highwayman's hitch.

The first horse Lincoln owned as an adult was probably the one he rode while serving in the Illinois militia during the Black Hawk War in 1832, when he was twenty-three. Lincoln rode the horse from his home in New Salem, near Springfield, up to the Michigan Territory, into what is now Wisconsin. He served less than three months and never saw combat. He later joked that he never "saw any live, fighting Indians . . . [but] had a good many bloody struggles with the mosquitoes." His horse was stolen in Whitewater, Wisconsin, the night before he was discharged, and Lincoln had to walk most of the way back home to New Salem.

Four years later, Lincoln lost another horse. This we know from a classified advertisement that appeared in the *Sangamo Journal* on March 26, 1836:

> STRAYED OR STOLEN, FROM a stable in Springfield, on Wednesday, 18th inst. a large bay horse, star in his forehead, plainly marked with harness, supposed to be eight years old; had been shod all round, but is believed to have lost some of his shoes, and trots and paces. Any person who will take up said horse, and leave information at the Journal office, or with the subscriber at New-salem, shall be liberally paid for their trouble. A. LINCOLN.

Losing a horse was no small inconvenience. They were expensive—a good one might set you back a hundred dollars or more, over $2,000 today—so they were frequently targeted by thieves. It's not known whether Lincoln ever got this horse back, but he probably didn't. Joshua Speed recalled that when Lincoln moved from New Salem to Springfield in 1837 he was riding a borrowed horse.

In fact, when Lincoln began riding the Illinois Eighth Circuit around 1840, he was still too poor to afford a horse, so he borrowed one from a friend named R. L. Wilson, who later complained that Lincoln "must have been careless, as the saddle skinned the horse's back." Eventually Lincoln procured a horse named Old Buck, who would be his companion on the circuit for many years, usually pulling a small buggy. Lincoln may have jokingly named the horse after James Buchanan, already a rising star in the Democratic Party, whose nickname was Old Buck. That tale is impossible to verify, of course, but it would certainly be in keeping with Lincoln's character.

Lincoln was still riding Old Buck to court in 1852, and Judge David Davis, who frequently presided over cases on Lincoln's circuit, recalled a three-day, seventy-mile ride that year, between Paris and Shelbyville: "My horses were very tired. Mr. Lincoln's old horse nearly gave out." Apparently Davis's son George was an occasional passenger in Lincoln's buggy. In a letter to the twelve-year-old boy in 1854, the judge wrote, "I write you in the midst of a trial, and while Mr. Gridley is talking to the Jury—to be followed by Mr. Lincoln. He recollects your ride with old Buck to Danville."

By 1855 the iron horse had replaced the real thing on the Eighth Circuit. Trains now connected Springfield to most county seats on the circuit. The old circuit riders practically became commuters. "Mr. Lincoln is with me & sends his love to you," Judge Davis wrote his son while on the circuit that year. "He says 'Old Buck' is alive. We don't use buggies so much in travelling since railroads have come in vogue."

During some fifteen years riding the circuit, Lincoln spent countless hours in very close contact with his horses. Inevitably a strong bond of affection developed between rider and horse, and Lincoln became very attached to his mounts. He fed and groomed them himself, and in time he became a skilled equestrian. Ulysses S. Grant recalled that Lincoln was "a fine horseman" who could easily handle Grant's favorite horse, Cincinnati.

Traveling the circuit also helped Lincoln forge personal and political relationships that would be critical to his career. Judge Davis, for example, would come to be one of his most important supporters. A newspaperman who traveled with Lincoln through central Illinois in 1847 said "it seemed as if . . . he had a kind word, a smile and a bow for every body on the road, even to the horses, and the cattle, and the swine."

Howard M. Powel (sometimes spelled "Powell," 1839–1917) probably knew Lincoln's horses about as well as Lincoln himself knew them. When Powel was twelve, his family moved from Philadelphia into a house next door to the Lincolns in Springfield. Lincoln hired the boy to sleep in the house while he was away on the circuit, because, as Powel explained, "Mrs. Lincoln was very nervous and subsequently

easily scared." Powel was paid five cents a night for his ser-
vices. Soon, driving Lincoln's horses was added to his duties.
"At first Mr. Lincoln had but one horse, a bay named Buck,"
Powel explained many years later.

> He bought another, however, from Thomas Bergen,
> paying $125 therefor—a good price in those days—
> and named the horse Tom for the man from whom
> he purchased it. . . . I would take Mrs. Lincoln &
> her friends riding in the afternoons. For this
> Mrs. Lincoln paid me five cents per hour. I do not
> know whether Mr. Lincoln kept an account of it or
> not but we never had a settlement. Whenever I
> wanted any money I would tell and he would ask
> how much.

The second horse allowed Mary to have transportation
while Lincoln was riding the circuit. Lincoln also purchased
a second buggy, making the Lincolns a "two-buggy" family—a sure sign of status in the frontier town. Occasionally, Lincoln would loan one of his horses to Joseph Kent,
another neighbor boy, so he could go swimming at Spring
Creek. On one occasion, Joseph summoned the courage to
ask Lincoln if he could borrow one of his buggies as well.
"Looking down on me with a broad smile of mirth," Kent
recalled, Lincoln said, "No, Joseph, there is two things I will
not loan, my wife and my carriage."

Howard Powel moved away from Springfield in the
autumn of 1853. Sometime thereafter Lincoln acquired a
new bay horse. Lincoln named the horse Robin, though

he came to be called Old Bob, to distinguish him from Lincoln's eldest son, "young" Bob. Old Bob likely replaced Old Buck, who was more than fifteen years old and due for retirement. Perhaps Old Buck died naturally; perhaps he was sold for parts, as it were: aged horses at that time were often rendered.

As with all his horses, Lincoln kept Tom and Old Bob stabled in the barn behind the house. As the newer horse, Old Bob became Lincoln's primary mount, relegating Tom to backup status.

Returning home after a long journey, Lincoln would carefully inspect Old Bob's hooves and stroke him tenderly. His affection for the animal was plain, and a neighbor once remarked that Lincoln "loved his horse well."

One visitor to Springfield described Old Bob as a "splendid old horse of dark bay color with swelling nostrils and eyes of an eagle." That description was perhaps a bit overwrought. Others said the horse was "pretty" but a bit swaybacked.

A HORSE CAN NEVER ENTER A HOME, of course, so Tom and Old Bob, no matter how much time they spent with their master, could never be more than part of the extended family.

So, by Christmas 1855, Fido was clearly the king of the castle on Eighth and Jackson. Though he surely spent much of his time in the barn with the other animals, he was also given free rein of the house, allowed inside whenever he wished, even if his paws were dirty. His favorite piece of furniture was a seven-foot-long horsehair sofa that Lincoln had had custom made to accommodate his six-foot-four frame. Atop it, Fido napped. Beneath it, he sought refuge during thunderstorms or when fireworks and cannons were set off during community celebrations.

IT IS WELL ESTABLISHED THAT PETS, especially dogs, can have a positive effect on people who suffer mental health problems, including mood disorders like the "hypo." A 2009 study in the *American Journal of Orthopsychiatry* concluded that "pets assist individuals in recovery from serious mental illness by":

(a) providing empathy and "therapy";
(b) providing connections that can assist in redeveloping social avenues;
(c) serving as "family" in the absence of or in addition to human family members; and
(d) supporting self-efficacy and strengthening a sense of empowerment.

"Pets appear to provide more benefits than merely companionship," the study found. "Participants' reports of pet-related contributions to their well-being provide impetus to conduct more formal research on the mechanisms by which pets contribute to recovery and to develop pet-based interventions."

We can't know whether Fido had anything to do with it, of course, but by the end of 1855, Lincoln's hypo was easing. His law practice was thriving once again. And he had decided to get back into politics.

2

1856

IF EVER THERE WAS A LUCKY DOG, it was Fido. In mid-nineteenth-century America, most stray animals—they were actually called tramps back then (and into the twentieth century, hence *Lady and the Tramp*)—were fated to short, miserable lives. Unlike tramp cats, which were known at least to control the vermin population, tramp dogs were considered a useless menace. They preyed on poultry and spread diseases. Ownerless dogs roaming the streets were regarded as a public health hazard. Efforts to cull the population were brutal but efficient. Police often were permitted to shoot stray dogs on sight. Many communities offered bounties for stray dogs each summer, perhaps a few cents a head, and boys and young men would spend their days wandering the streets, happily clubbing the animals to death for pocket change. Dogs with collars were exempted from these culls, so sympathetic humans might tie a bandana around a friendly tramp's neck to spare it this gory end.

The abolitionist Lydia Maria Child abhorred these kills, which she believed contributed to larger social problems. In 1841 she wrote about a cull she had witnessed in New York City:

Twelve or fifteen hundred of these animals have been killed this summer in the hottest of weather at a rate of three hundred a day. The safety of the city doubtless requires their expulsion; but the *manner* of it strikes me as exceedingly cruel and demoralizing. The poor creatures are knocked down on the pavement, and beat to death. Sometimes they are horribly maimed, and run howling and limping away. The company of dog-killers themselves are a frightful sight, with their bloody clubs and spattered garments. I always run from the window when I hear them; for they remind me of the Reign of Terror. Whether such brutal scenes do not prepare the minds of the young to take part in bloody riots and revolutions is a serious matter.

"Even routine control of strays in cities was done with considerable cruelty," wrote Katherine C. Grier in *Pets in America: A History*. "The contractors of city dog carts strangled their victims with wire lassos and sometimes clubbed or shot them on the spot, and frantic captured dogs often tore each other to pieces within the confines of the dog wagons."

Even if they survived this thinning of the herd, tramp dogs were likely to become ill, either from diseases like distemper or rabies, from wounds sustained in fights, or simply from the privations of living outside. Theirs was not a pleasant existence. Even the hardiest tramp dogs were lucky to survive just a few years.

Such was the fate that would have awaited Fido had Abraham Lincoln not rescued him from the streets of Springfield.

Fido's story might have been lost to history forever if not for the efforts of a remarkable woman named Dorothy Meserve Kunhardt (1901–79). Kunhardt was the daughter of Frederick Hill Meserve, a textile executive from New York who amassed the world's largest private collection of Lincoln and Civil War photographs. At the time of his death in 1962, Meserve owned approximately two hundred thousand images, including some ten thousand glass negatives from pioneering photographer Mathew Brady.

Dorothy inherited her father's love of all things Lincoln and proved to be a formidable Lincoln scholar in her own right. Indeed, she was a woman of many talents. In addition to her work on Lincoln, she also published more than a dozen children's books, including the classic *Pat the Bunny*. One of the first "touch and feel" books, it has sold more than six million copies since it was first published in 1940. Her son, Philip B. Kunhardt Jr., recalled that growing up with such a brilliant mother could be exasperating:

> How could she possibly run a home with so many obsessions stirring around in her heart, so many interests whirring around in her head—interest in anything old, in every animal in the world, in Indians, in medicine, in photographs, in Abraham Lincoln, in slaves, in spiritualism, in subways, in freaks, in crime, in death, in love—the list went on and on, growing longer with each new carload of books she brought home from the secondhand dealer.

One day in the 1930s, while researching a book on Lincoln's son Tad, Dorothy Kunhardt was searching through her

father's collection of photographs when she came upon an
image that stuck out to her:

> As I held old collodion negatives up to the light and
> went through cabinet after cabinet crammed with
> pictures of the period, I came upon the photograph
> of a dog mixed in with the impressive likenesses
> of Army officers. There was something curiously
> moving about this rough-coated, stubby-tailed lit-
> tle animal, stiffly posed and, I thought, obviously
> trying desperately to obey the order to hold still.

This intersection of two of her great loves—Lincoln and
animals—would prove irresistible to Kunhardt, and over the
next several years she managed to track down a handful of
the Lincoln family's friends and neighbors to inquire about
the animal. In 1940 she interviewed Isaac Diller, son of the
proprietor of Diller's drugstore and one of Willie and Tad's
playmates. At the time, Diller, who was eighty-six, was the
last living person known to have been photographed with
Lincoln. He happened to be standing in front of the Lincoln home one day in 1860 when a photographer snapped
a picture of Lincoln in the yard with Willie and Tad. Unfortunately for little Isaac—and, according to Kunhardt, "to
his lifelong chagrin"—he turned his head to look at a passing wagon at the moment the shutter was opened. In the
photograph the upper half of his body is only a blur, like a
pixelated face in a modern reality TV show.

   Isaac Diller identified the stubby-tailed little animal
Kunhardt inquired about as Abraham Lincoln's dog Fido.

Diller then referred Kunhardt to another friend of Willie and Tad's, John Linden Roll, also eighty-six at the time. Roll was the son of John Eddy Roll, one of Lincoln's oldest friends in Springfield. Their recollections helped Kunhardt "piece together" the Fido story, which she would publish in the February 15, 1954, issue of *Life* magazine. The *Life* article is the urtext for Fido researchers (admittedly a small bunch).

Three photographs of Fido are known to exist. All seem to have been taken at the same sitting in a photographic

PRESIDENT LINCOLN'S DOG.

PRESIDENT LINCOLN'S DOG.

PIETZ, 1858 No. 201 South 6th St., SPRINGFIELD, ILLS.

These are the only photographs of Fido known to exist. All three were taken in a single sitting at a studio in Springfield, though the precise date of the session is uncertain.
ABRAHAM LINCOLN PRESIDENTIAL LIBRARY AND MUSEUM (ALPLM)

studio. (The precise date of these images is very much in dispute.) In all three photographs Fido is shown atop a washstand that has been covered with a decorated cloth or perhaps a piece of carpeting. Two of the images are nearly identical: Fido is shown in profile, facing left and lying flat. His front paws are draped over the left edge of the washstand. His back legs are tucked underneath him. His short, bushy tail is sticking straight out behind him. In one of the poses his head is low, and blurry, the effect of his moving, like little Isaac Diller, while the shutter was open. In the other his head is slightly raised and in better focus.

The third pose is different. Fido, now turned toward the camera, is seated comfortably, leaning slightly to his right, his paws dangling casually over the front of the washstand. In this image he is clearly more comfortable than in the other two, in which his body seems almost rigid. Perhaps this was the final shot, and Fido had grown more relaxed. In any event, he seems to be enjoying himself: unlike in the other two photos, his tail is limp, resting on the washstand.

"He looks every inch a trustworthy and dependable pet who took the responsibilities of his position as Family Dog very seriously," wrote Ruth Painter Randall in *Lincoln's Animal Friends*. "Looking at his picture, you feel sure he watched carefully over Willie and Tad, his unpredictable little masters, and kept a wary eye out for tramps, burglars, and other undesirable characters."

Much debate has surrounded the issue of Fido's pedigree, of which we know nothing for certain. These images offer the only clues. Some have guessed that he was a shepherd/ retriever mix. Melinda Merck, a forensic veterinarian who examined the Fido photographs in 2013, believes he was "predominantly Labrador retriever."

It suffices to say that Fido was a good old American mutt—a mongrel, to use a word from the period, a term then fraught with ugly weight. And one thing's for sure: Fido was one pampered pooch. Merck said the dog in the three images looks remarkably healthy, especially considering the times in which he lived: "coat looks great, clean, smooth; bright eyes."

Much more is known about Fido's personality than his pedigree. Like many dogs, he loved to chase his own tail. This amused Lincoln to no end, and he never tired of watching Fido spin furiously in a perpetually fruitless attempt to catch the stubby protuberance on his backside. Fido was probably the inspiration for one of Lincoln's favorite riddles:

"If you call a tail a leg," he'd say, "how many legs does a dog have?"

"Five!" would come the inevitable answer.

"No," Lincoln would reply. "Calling a tail a leg don't make it a leg."

Something else we know about Fido's personality: He liked to jump up on people. Lincoln's old friend John Eddy Roll, father of Willie and Tad's playmates Frank and John Linden Roll, described Fido in an 1893 interview with the *Illinois State Journal*:

Fido had some of the qualities which characterized his master, in so far as a dumb [i.e., mute] animal can resemble in disposition a human being. He was exceptionally friendly and had a habit of showing his congeniality by depositing his muddy yellow fore paws plump on the breast of any one who addressed him familiarly.

Roll wasn't kidding about the muddy forepaws. "Springfield was famous for the wretched conditions of its streets," one local historian wrote, betraying just a hint of pride in this notoriety. The roads were unpaved, and when it rained they turned into "prairie gumbo," a mud so deep and thick that horses often got stuck in it. Sometimes the muck even trapped oxen. "It was no infrequent thing," one old-timer recalled many years later, "to see four horses attached to one carriage and even then with great difficulty were the passengers able to arrive at their destination."

One visitor alleged that nobody "can know the definition of 'Mud' until they come to Springfield."

According to Ruth Painter Randall, "There was the question whether getting on the boys' clean bed with muddy feet was justified by the comfort [Fido's] warm, loving body gave to the bed's small occupants." But she concluded, "Since the Lincolns believed in letting the children have a good time, you can be sure Fido stayed on the bed."

While Fido may have been "showing his congeniality" by jumping up on people, he was also making them dirty. Regarded by most as nothing more than an annoying habit, in time this would lead to Fido's undoing.

Judging by his name, we can assume Fido was an extremely loyal dog, for "Fido" derives from *fidelitas*, the Latin word for faithful. It was a common name for pet dogs at the time, but eventually, largely due to Lincoln's Fido, it would practically become a generic term for all dogs. The most popular name for male dogs in the mid-nineteenth century was probably Carlo, after the faithful pointer in *Jane Eyre*. For female dogs it was Jenny Lind, after the famous Swedish opera singer who toured the United States in the early 1850s.

WHEN ABRAHAM LINCOLN decided to plunge back into politics in early 1856, he faced a problem: he didn't have a political party. All his adult life, Lincoln had belonged to the Whigs, a party founded in the early 1830s to oppose the policies of Democratic president Andrew Jackson. The Whigs favored a strong central government, compulsory public education, and internal improvements, such as roads and canals.

For a time the party was quite successful. Two Whigs were elected president, William Henry Harrison in 1840 and Zachary Taylor in 1848. But in what can only be considered a bad omen for the party's future, both men died in office. Harrison, who at sixty-eight was the oldest president until Ronald Reagan, famously caught a cold while delivering, without a hat or overcoat on a frigid day, the longest inauguration speech in history—it lasted nearly two hours. The cold he caught on Inauguration Day may or may not have contributed to the pneumonia that killed him just thirty-one days later. For his part, poor old Zack Taylor died of dysentery only sixteen months after taking office, possibly after consuming tainted milk.

By the mid-1850s, the Whigs were hopelessly split on the slavery question. Northern Whigs either supported outright abolition or, like Lincoln, at least opposed the extension of slavery. Southern Whigs were proslavery. Their differences proved irreconcilable, so, inconceivable as it seems today, one of the country's two major political parties simply disintegrated, shattered by its failure to agree on the single most pressing political issue of the day, namely the propriety of human bondage. (The Democratic Party had to cope with its own schism over slavery, though there were enough Northern Democrats with Southern sympathies—known as "doughfaces"—to keep the party together, at least until the 1860 presidential election. The two presidents immediately preceding Lincoln, Franklin Pierce and James Buchanan, were both Northern Democrats who accommodated the South.)

Lincoln himself felt abandoned by the Whigs. "You enquire where I now stand," Lincoln wrote his old friend Joshua Speed. "That is a disputed point. I think I am a whig; but others say there are no whigs, and that I am an abolitionist." Lincoln, however, was no abolitionist and quickly reminded his friend, "I now do no more than oppose the *extension* of slavery." Lincoln was willing to "tolerate" the peculiar institution where it already existed. "The framers of the Constitution found the institution of slavery amongst their other institutions at the time," Lincoln said. "They found that by an effort to eradicate it, they might lose much of what they had already gained [by winning independence]. They were obliged to bow to the necessity." Containing slavery, Lincoln believed, would cause it to ultimately disappear.

While Southern Whigs flocked to the proslavery wing of the Democratic Party, antislavery Northern Whigs were left politically homeless. Adrift, they decided to join with like-minded Northern Democrats and others opposed to slavery (or its extension) to form a new party, which in time came to be known as the Republican Party.

Though he opposed the expansion of slavery, Lincoln would hardly be considered enlightened on racial matters by today's standards. He harbored no convictions that blacks were equal to whites in all respects—only that they were, in the words of the Declaration of Independence, "created equal." Lincoln once said he believed the Founding Fathers never intended "to say all were equal in color, size, intellect, moral developments, or social capacity." Indeed, Lincoln's own solution to the slavery problem was as quixotic as it was untenable: repatriation. He belonged to an organization called the American Colonization Society, which advocated "repatriating" African Americans to Liberia. (He once served on the board of directors of the organization's Illinois branch.) Supporters of this proposal believed Southern slaveholders would be more willing to relinquish their slaves, either voluntarily or for cash payments, if the freed slaves were shipped back to Africa instead of being permitted to remain in America, where they would disrupt the social order. Voluntary deportation, Lincoln believed, would succeed in "restoring a captive people to their long-lost fatherland, with bright prospects for the future." (Never mind that the Atlantic slave trade had been outlawed in 1808, so most slaves in the United States had never set foot in Africa.) Some supporters of colonization were motivated by simple racism. Ohio senator Ben Wade said the plan would "rid ourselves of these people" and end, once and for all, talk of "negro equality or anything of that kind."

But the dream of somehow repatriating African Americans to their "long-lost fatherland" died with the Kansas-Nebraska Act of 1854. Rather than pressing slaveholders to manumit their slaves for relocation, the law encouraged them to expand their empire of human misery by extending slavery into the territories. Proslavery forces flooded into Kansas (including many from neighboring Missouri, a slave state) and established a farcical government that not only legalized slavery in the territory but also made it a capital offense to speak out against it.

Antislavery groups set up a competing (and equally spurious) government in the territory. Conflict was inevitable. The divide in Kansas neatly reflected the broader divide in the country as a whole and foreshadowed the impending war between the states. On May 19 and 20, 1856, Massachusetts senator Charles Sumner delivered a long speech on the Senate floor in which he called for Kansas to be admitted to the Union immediately as a free state, and denounced efforts to impose slavery there as "the rape of a virgin Territory." Sumner heaped special scorn on Senator Andrew Butler of South Carolina, one of the architects of the Kansas-Nebraska Act:

> The senator from South Carolina has read many books of chivalry, and believes himself a chivalrous knight with sentiments of honor and courage. Of course he has chosen a mistress to whom he has made his vows, and who, though ugly to others, is always lovely to him; though polluted in the sight of the world, is chaste in his sight—I mean the harlot, slavery.

Sumner's speech, replete with vivid sexual imagery and the mockery of Southern values, was sure to draw an angry response. Two days later, it did. While sitting at his desk on the Senate floor, Sumner was approached by Preston Brooks, a congressman from South Carolina and Senator Butler's cousin. Telling Sumner his speech was "a libel on South Carolina, and Mr. Butler, who is a relative of mine," Brooks raised a heavy cane and brought it down on Sumner's head. Brooks continued beating Sumner over the head until he was unconscious. He didn't stop until the cane broke into pieces. Sumner's injuries were so severe that he would not return to the Senate permanently for three years. (Brooks survived a motion to expel him from the House but died unexpectedly of croup less than a year after attacking Sumner. He was thirty-seven. Brooks County, Georgia, is named in his honor.)

The vicious attack on Sumner—at his desk on the Senate floor, no less—galvanized opponents of slavery and helped coalesce the nascent Republican Party.

On Thursday, May 29, 1856, exactly one week after the attack on Sumner, Abraham Lincoln and some 270 other delegates convened in Bloomington, Illinois, to formally organize the Illinois Republican Party. As in other states, Illinois Republicans were a loose alliance of radical abolitionists, antislavery Democrats, old conservative Whigs, and members of the rabid anti-immigrant and anti-Catholic party known as the Know Nothings (because their secretive members professed to know nothing about the party when asked). What united them was their virulent opposition to the expansion of slavery, the attack on Senator Sumner, and recent violence in Kansas, where a proslavery militia had attacked the antislavery community of Lawrence.

In this ragtag coalition, a crude amalgamation of disparate groups, Lincoln saw an opportunity. What the new party needed in Illinois was a leader, and Lincoln was determined to fill this vacancy. "Lincoln was the master spirit of the convention," wrote Michael Burlingame in his monumental Lincoln biography, "managing through some political alchemy to convince former enemies to set aside their differences and cooperate for the greater good." Though the party did not nominate Lincoln to run for any office, he was universally recognized as the de facto leader of the Republican Party in Illinois.

With a presidential election coming up, Lincoln threw himself into organizing the party. Visitors called on him at home almost constantly. Fido must've wondered who these strangers were who kept interrupting his naps on the long horsehair sofa to pat his head or stroke his coarse yellow coat. He was a friendly dog, though he must have resented these visitors for commanding so much of his master's time.

WHILE IT SEEMS QUAINT, EVEN ROMANTIC, to say that Abraham Lincoln was born in a log cabin, the fact is that his childhood was one of constant privation. He once described his early life by quoting Thomas Gray's "Elegy Written in a Country Churchyard": "The short and simple annals of the poor." His peripatetic father, Thomas Lincoln, a farmer and sometime carpenter, searched constantly for greener pastures, literally and figuratively. Thomas had moved from Virginia to Kentucky with his family in 1780, when he was only about four years old. (At the time, Kentucky was still part of Virginia; it became the fifteenth state in 1792.)

In 1806 Thomas married Nancy Hanks, who, like Thomas, had moved west with her family at a young age. Eight months after their wedding, their first child, a daughter named Sarah, was born. Two years after that, on February 12, 1809, Abraham Lincoln was born in a windowless, dirt-floored cabin on the south fork of Nolin Creek, near the town of Hodgenville, in central Kentucky. One person who saw the cabin remembered it as a "miserable habitation." By the time Abraham was two, the family had moved about ten miles away, to a similar cabin on Knob Creek. Here were formed young Lincoln's first memories.

Life on the frontier was hard and the Lincoln family's circumstances were meager, so Abraham was expected to pull his weight from a very early age. As a result he received little formal education. He would later estimate that the sum of all his schooling "did not amount to one year." Of what little schooling he received, Lincoln was scornful. "No qualification was ever required of a teacher," he once said. However, as his biographer David Herbert Donald has pointed out, "a school system that produced Abraham Lincoln could not have been wholly without merit."

By the time he was six, in 1815, he was helping his father plant pumpkin seeds and was regularly assigned tasks such as fetching water and collecting firewood. It was likely on one of these errands that Abe visited a neighboring farm, where a litter of striped piglets had recently been born.

"You may have one of those pigs if you can get him home," the neighbor told Abe. This "filled me with supreme joy," Lincoln told a friend more than forty years later. "I instantly accepted the offer." Abe wrapped the animal in his shirt and hurried back to the cabin on Knob Creek. With cornhusks and leaves, he carefully fashioned a cradle for the baby pig inside a hollow log.

Over the next several months, the future president and the pig became best friends. "That pig," Lincoln said, "was my companion."

> After awhile he got too heavy for me to carry around, and then he followed me everywhere—to the barn, to the plowed ground, and to the woods. Many a day I spent in the woods, brushing the leaves away, picking out the most promising spots, helping him to find acorns and nuts. Sometimes he would have a lazy spell. Then he would rub against my legs, and stop in front of me, and lie down in a sort of wheedling way, and say, in the language which I understood, "Abe, why don't you carry me, the same as you used to?"

Eventually the pig grew very large—"too large for his own good and mine," as Lincoln put it. Little Abe began to hear talk around the house that the pig was now fat enough to kill. Given the family's limited means, this was hardly a radical denouement, but young Lincoln was devastated. It was, he said, "the beginning of a tragedy to me." He awoke one morning and was horrified to discover that his father had built a spit on which to cook the pig.

"I was suddenly seized with a determination to save my playmate," Lincoln recalled.

I slipped out and took him with me into the woods. When father found what had happened he yelled as loud as he could:

"You, Abe, fetch back that hog! You, Abe, fetch back that hog!"

The louder father called the further and faster we went, till we were out of hearing of the voice. We stayed in the woods till night. On returning I was severely scolded. Father and mother explained to me that we could not keep the hog through the winter for me to play with—that hogs were meant to be killed for food. I was not convinced.

Abe awoke early the next morning to hide in the woods with his pet for another day. But his father had awakened even earlier, and the pig was secured in a pen. "I knew then," Lincoln said, "there was no hope for my pig."

Abe ran into the woods. "I had not got far into the woods before I heard the pig squeal, and I ran faster than ever to get away from the sound."

Being quite hungry at midday, I started for home. Reaching the edge of the clearing, I saw the hog, dressed, hanging from the pole near the barn. I began to blubber. I just couldn't reconcile myself to my loss. I could not stand it, and went far back into the woods again, where I found some nuts that satisfied my hunger till night, when I returned home.

They could not get me to take any of the meat;
neither tenderloin, nor sausage, nor souse; and even
months after, when the cured ham came on the
table, it made me sad and sick to look at it.

This unsettling event—an "awful tragedy," as Lincoln
later described it—was a common childhood experience in
the nineteenth century, when many families, even in the
largest cities, kept livestock. "Townspeople often kept flocks
of chickens or a pig or two," Katherine C. Grier, author of
Pets in America: A History, has pointed out. "Both working-
and middle-class families kept a family cow and made extra
income by sharing milk with their neighbors." The children
in families that kept livestock often became quite attached
to the animals, creating unpleasant dilemmas for both the
children and their parents.

In 1963 the novelist Mary Ellen Chase published a
children's book called *Victoria: A Pig in a Pram* in which
she recalled a traumatic pig incident from her childhood
that was remarkably similar to young Abe Lincoln's. In
1897 ten-year-old Mary Ellen rescued an injured piglet
from the sty under a barn on her family's farm in Blue
Hill, Maine. The animal's back had been broken when its
mother rolled over on it. Chase named the piglet Victoria
and, with her mother's help, nursed it back to health. She
made a bed for Victoria in a laundry basket, fed her oat-
meal, and bathed her daily. Chase would sometimes dress
Victoria in a bonnet and booties and push her around
the town in a pram. The little girl and her pet piglet were
inseparable.

But as Victoria grew into a plump hog, much too heavy for Chase to carry, the future novelist began to worry about what the days ahead held for her porcine companion.

"I only wish she weren't growing quite so fast!" her mother would say, ominously, of the fattening pig.

"Somewhere in the dim future I sensed tragedy," Chase wrote, "but I resolutely put all such dark fears out of my mind."

> I did this in much the way that one watches thunder-clouds roll up in the western sky and then sees them mercifully move on to crash their thunder and to flash their lightning over other houses, other orchards, other children.

When her father declared one day that Victoria was "reverting to type," Chase's older sister Edith had to explain to her exactly what he meant. "He meant that she's just a pig after all," Edith said. "He meant she'd become just like her family if you put her down with them under the barn." He also meant it was time for Victoria to serve her true purpose in life: to become food. It was, Mary Ellen's mother explained, "just the way things are." At least the young girl was spared the sight of her pet pig on a serving tray. Her parents sold Victoria to a neighbor and sent Mary Ellen on an errand when he came to fetch the pig.

In 1878 an eleven-year-old girl from Massachusetts named Margaret Harding Tileston began keeping a diary (a practice she would continue until her death from pneumonia at thirty-four). Margaret had a habit of naming the animals on her family's farm in Concord. One of her favorites was a calf she named Brighteyes. Margaret considered Brighteyes a pet and called her "the sweetest bossie that ever was born."

On February 5, 1879, Margaret wrote in her diary:

> Tomorrow the butcher is coming to take my Bright-eyes away. . . . I have planted a great many kisses on the pretty white star in Brighteyes forhed [*sic*]. She will always be a dear, little calf in Heaven.

"The butcher came at six-oclock," Margaret wrote the next day. "I was awake in the night."

These heartbreaking experiences were expected to teach children a lesson: animals were inferior beings. According to this pedagogy, animals were put on the earth to serve humans. God said so, as recorded in Genesis 1:26: "Let us make man in our image, after our likeness: and let them have dominion over the fish of the sea, and over the fowl of the air, and over the cattle, and over all the earth, and over every creeping thing that creepeth upon the earth."

This, of course, was not a uniquely Judeo-Christian concept. The ancient Greeks also believed that nonhuman animals were inferior. According to Aristotle, "Plants exist for the sake of animals, and brute beasts for the sake of man—domestic animals for his use and food, wild ones (or at any rate most of them) for food and other accessories of life, such as clothing and various tools."

Two years after her beloved bossie was butchered, Margaret Harding Tileston, now fourteen years old, was put in charge of caring for her family's flock of chickens. As was her custom, she named the animals. But she had come to accept the prevailing ethos. "White Knight, Young Man and his twin brother, three of our cocks, were killed at night," Margaret wrote in her diary one day in January 1881. "We ate the three cocks for dinner and they were very nice and tender." Margaret no longer doubted the way things were.

Abraham Lincoln, however, never lost his empathy for animals—especially pigs.

When he was first elected to the Illinois General Assembly in 1834, Lincoln bought his first proper suit, at a cost of sixty dollars, a fantastic sum for him at the time. It was one of his most prized possessions. We don't know precisely what the suit looked like, but it probably resembled what other young men striving to be fashionable wore at the time: long trousers, a long-tailed coat, a vest, a fine white shirt, and a silk neckerchief or cravat.

Also around this time Lincoln began wearing his trademark stovepipe hat, an affectation that he would maintain for the rest of his life. By the early 1800s, wrote Debbie Henderson in *The Top Hat: An Illustrated History of Its Styling and Manufacture*, tall hats "had become the irrepressible symbol of prestige and authority." According to the Lincoln scholar Harold Holzer, "Hats were important to Lincoln: They protected him against inclement weather, served as storage bins for important papers he stuck inside their lining, and further accentuated his great height advantage over other men."

One day Lincoln was riding through the country, all fixed up in his new suit, when he came across a young pig stuck in thick, black mud. The more the animal struggled to free itself, the deeper it sank. As Lincoln approached on his

This statue of Lincoln and a pig was erected in Taylorville, Illinois, in 2005. Legend has it that Lincoln was arguing a case in the town's courthouse one day when some pigs that had managed to burrow underneath the building began squealing loudly. Jokingly, Lincoln asked the judge for a "writ of quietus" to silence them. COURTESY OF JEROME POHLEN

horse, the helpless swine looked up into his eyes, seemingly beseeching him for help. But Lincoln was in a hurry—and besides, he could not bear to ruin his new suit. He passed the stuck pig by, but his conscience would not allow him to go very far before he turned back.

"The poor pig looked at him 'wistfully,' as if he were saying to himself, '*there, now! My last hope is gone,*'" wrote Ruth Painter Randall in *Lincoln's Animal Friends*. "Abraham was lost; he could not stand that look in the animal's eyes. What if this had been his pet pig he had loved so much when he was a little boy? He got off his horse. Down he went into the mud, good clothes and all, and worked until he had that pig free again."

Many years later, when he was a successful lawyer in Springfield, Lincoln went for a long walk into the country with a friend one evening. As they strolled down a quiet lane, the two came upon six tiny piglets huddled with their noses close together. "Those little pigs are lost," Lincoln said. "Let's help them find their mother." The two men herded the piglets down the road until they discovered a hole in a barnyard fence. In the yard they could see a big, fat mother pig. The piglets scurried through the hole for a joyous reunion with their mother. Lincoln smiled. "I never see a pig," he said, "that I do not think of my first pet."

SPRINGFIELD IN THE 1850S was a community in transition. After the capital was moved from Vandalia to Springfield in 1839—largely due to Lincoln's maneuverings as a state lawmaker—Springfield began to boom. The population doubled between 1850 and 1860, from about forty-five hundred to nine thousand.

Despite its status as the state capital, however, Springfield was still very much a country town in the 1850s. Hogs and cattle roamed the unpaved streets. Public water and sewer systems had not yet been constructed, and cholera outbreaks were frequent and often fatal. A public school system "for the education of all white persons between the ages of five and twenty-one" was established in 1854, but it would not be fully operational for another four years. A separate school for "colored children" was established in 1855.

In May 1855 a new gas system began operating, and slowly the flicker of candlelight gave way to the hiss of gas lamps in homes and businesses. The number of policemen in the town rose from one to six during the decade, though the officers were, to their consternation, required to purchase their own uniforms.

"It would be very beautiful here if the streets were paved," wrote Frithjof Meidell, a Norwegian immigrant living in Springfield, in a letter to relatives. "But picture to yourself a town laid out on the blackest mold without pavement; add to this that swine, Irishmen, cows and Germans walk around loose in this slush and you have a pretty good idea how the streets look." A visitor in 1853 wrote, "Just think of a city containing seven or eight thousand inhabitants, with all the boasted wealth of this city, and so favorably patronized too, without a single good sidewalk in it, or even a public lamp to light a street!" (By the end of the decade, the town would install streetlamps and wooden sidewalks.)

Springfield emphatically embodied mid-nineteenth century American values. An 1851 ordinance forbade women from "appearing in slacks on the streets." Violators were guilty of a misdemeanor, punishable by a fine of "not less than three nor more than $100."

Springfield in 1865. The town was notorious for its mud. COURTESY OF LIBRARY OF CONGRESS

The decade's most popular songs, bought as sheet music and played on parlor pianos, were "De Camptown Races" and "My Old Kentucky Home," both composed by Stephen Foster, the 1850s version of Barry Manilow.

THE YEAR 1856 BROUGHT a three-way race for US president: John C. Frémont, an explorer and war hero, was the Republican nominee. James Buchanan, a former secretary of state, was the Democratic nominee; and former president Millard Fillmore ran as the Know Nothing candidate. Lincoln feared that Frémont and Fillmore would split the antislavery vote, handing the election to Buchanan. He hoped to secure

Illinois for the Republicans by winning over Fillmore's supporters to the Republican side.

Lincoln campaigned hard. That fall he gave some fifty
speeches for the Republican ticket all over Illinois. He tried
to convince his old Whig friends that a vote for Fillmore was
really a vote for Buchanan. "This is as plain as the adding up
of the weights of three small hogs," he told them. But his
valiant efforts were for naught. As he feared, the antislavery
vote was divided between Frémont and Fillmore. Buchanan
carried Illinois and won the election.

All was not lost, however: the fledgling Republican
Party won all the statewide offices in Illinois, including the
governorship.

3

1857

A FEW DAYS BEFORE HIS EIGHTH BIRTHDAY on February 12, 1817, Abraham Lincoln shot and killed a wild turkey outside his family's log cabin in Spencer County, Indiana. He had hoped to impress his father with his marksmanship, but the sight of the dead bird only left him traumatized, much like the sight of his pet pig dressed and hanging from a pole two years earlier. After shooting that turkey, he later wrote, he never again "pulled a trigger on any larger game."

Growing up in the wilds of Kentucky and Indiana, young Lincoln was compelled to hunt small game like possums, rabbits, raccoons, and squirrels. He found this requirement of frontier life unsavory. There is no evidence that he ever hunted at all as an adult; a friend remembered that he "took no interest in fishing-rod or gun." In the 1830s, when he was in his twenties and serving in the Illinois legislature, then located in Vandalia, some of his fellow lawmakers invited Lincoln to go deer hunting with them. Lincoln refused. "You go get the deer, Mattox [the proprietor of the hotel where the lawmakers were staying] can cook it and I'll eat all you can get."

His aversion to hunting did not preclude him from eating meat, however. Lincoln was not a vegetarian, as some animal rights groups have since claimed. One soiree at the Lincoln home in Springfield featured a table "loaded with venison, wild turkeys, prairie chickens, quails, and other game."

Young Abraham Lincoln was raised in a culture inoculated against concern for animals. On the frontier, animals were considered nothing more than tools for human progress. They were sources of both labor and nourishment. They were also a source of amusement in an environment otherwise bereft of diversions from the backbreaking drudgery of everyday life.

When Lincoln was growing up, animal cruelty was a form of entertainment. One popular pastime was gander pulling. It was simple, really: a live goose was hung upside down from a high tree limb. Then riders on horseback took turns galloping under the helpless, hanging bird, reaching up to snatch off its head. Whoever successfully decapitated the bird was the "winner."

Dogfighting was also popular, of course, as were cockfighting and bear baiting, in which hunting dogs were set upon a bear tied to a tree. Starved lions in traveling menageries were fed live cats and dogs, which they tore to pieces for the enjoyment of paying customers. This casual cruelty was partly the result of what historian Katherine C. Grier has called the "rough world of male privilege that regarded the suffering of the powerless as a joke." Grier cites William Otter (1787–1856), a tavern keeper in Pennsylvania and Maryland, who recounted a litany of blithe acts of animal cruelty in his memoir: drowning an immigrant's pet dog as a joke, stuffing a live turkey down a chimney, running a herd of horses to the brink of death, scalding a monkey on a hot stove.

Children were no less cruel to animals than adults. Boys playing war games sometimes hanged "traitorous" cats and dogs from tree limbs. Lads were also known to set cats on fire for fun. Lincoln himself witnessed such wanton cruelty when he was a young boy. One day he saw some boys putting hot coals on the back of a turtle, which struggled awkwardly and vainly to escape the torment. It was a pastime known as "teasin' tarrypins," and the boys laughed heartily at the spectacle. Young Lincoln intervened and rescued the helpless turtle. Another time he admonished his friends that "an ant's life was to it as sweet as ours to us."

Still another instance of cruelty involved Abe's first pet dog. When he was six or seven years old and still living at Knob Creek, Abe came to own a pup named Honey. Legend has it that the dog had a broken leg when Lincoln found him. Young Abe carried the dog to a nearby cave and brought the injured animal food and water every day for several weeks until he was well enough to bring home. It's also possible that Abe's parents gave him the dog to compensate for the loss of his pet pig.

Honey, who was probably named for his yellowish coat, became Abe's constant companion, accompanying his young master on long trips into the woods to fish, hunt, and fetch firewood. Sometimes Honey would chase a rabbit into a hollow log or tree and Abe would use his axe to chop it out. On many of these trips, Abe and Honey were accompanied by Abe's friend Austin Gollaher, whose family lived about two miles from the Lincoln cabin. One day, Abe, Honey, and Austin were walking home when they came upon a drunk man staggering down the road. Honey, perhaps sensing something sinister about the drunk, started barking. The man became enraged and began kicking the dog as hard as he could. The boys were too small to intervene. Helpless, Abe screamed in rage. Tears rolled down his cheeks. This would be the only time Austin ever saw his friend lose control of his emotions. Eventually the boys were able to scoop up the dog and race home before the drunk could catch them, and Abe nursed Honey back to health.

Austin Gollaher, incidentally, deserves credit for saving Abraham Lincoln's life. On another of their expeditions, the boys came upon a creek that was swollen and too wide for them to jump across. Gollaher remembered the incident many years later:

Finally, we saw a narrow foot-log, and we concluded to try it. It was narrow, but Abe said, "Let's coon it."

I went first and reached the other side all right. Abe went about half-way across, when he got scared and began trembling. I hollered to him, "Don't look down nor up nor sideways, but look right at me and hold on tight!" But he fell off into the creek, and, as the water was about seven or eight feet deep, and I could not swim, and neither could Abe, I knew it would do no good for me to go in after him.

So I got a stick—a long water sprout—and held it out to him. He came up, grabbed with both hands, and I put the stick into his hands. He clung to it, and I pulled him out on the bank, almost dead. I got him by the arms and shook him well, and then rolled him on the ground, when the water poured out of his mouth.

He was all right very soon. We promised each other that we would never tell anybody about it, and never did for years. I never told any one of it until after Lincoln was killed.

For the early settlers of what was then the western frontier, life was hard, with little margin for error. So perhaps they can be forgiven for their seemingly callous attitude toward animals. An animal's life was of little concern in the grand scheme of things, its welfare a concern only insofar as it impacted human welfare. A lame horse, after all, was useless for transportation. A sick cow might produce toxic milk. Lincoln's own mother died from drinking tainted milk when he was just nine years old. That he grew up in such an environment makes young Abraham Lincoln's empathy for animals all the more extraordinary; his love of animals was remarkably progressive—even eccentric.

One biographer, David Herbert Donald, has speculated that the death of Lincoln's mother may have had something to do with his aversion to cruelty and bloodshed. (Others have also suggested that his mother's death may have contributed to Lincoln's episodes of depression later in life.) During one of his brief stints attending school, Abe was assigned to write an essay. The topic he chose was animal cruelty. The essay itself has not survived, unfortunately, but even many years later, his schoolmates remembered it well.

After Nancy Lincoln died, Abe's father married Sarah Bush Johnston, a widow whom he had known years before in Kentucky. Sarah brought to the marriage her three children, two girls and a boy—and, according to Lincoln biographer Albert Beveridge, a pet cat. Sarah "proved to be a good and kind mother," Lincoln recalled. But to eleven-year-old Abe, the cat was more exciting than a new ma. One of Lincoln's chores was to fetch water from a spring about a mile away from the family's cabin. This he did at least once a day, and the cat accompanied him every time.

Lincoln, of course, was no Saint Francis of Assisi. Even he had to defer to the realities of life on the frontier. For a time in his late teens, he earned money by slaughtering hogs, a job he surely detested. Still, he was at the vanguard of what would become the animal welfare movement.

LINCOLN'S LOVE OF ANIMALS was nurtured by his love of books. As a boy, he could not afford to purchase his own, of course, so he borrowed them from friends and neighbors. His mother and, later, his stepmother both encouraged his bibliophilic tendencies, but his uneducated father could not appreciate this facet of Abe's personality. There was work to be done: clearing fields, plowing, planting, hunting. Often Lincoln's father would find his son reading instead of working, infuriating the elder Lincoln, who felt reading for pleasure was a luxury the family could not afford.

But Lincoln was undeterred. He was an autodidact, and through books he taught himself science, politics, philosophy, religion, and law. When a law student wrote Lincoln asking for advice in 1855, Lincoln answered, "Get the books, and read and study them."

Books also taught Lincoln about animal welfare. As a young man, Lincoln read Thomas Paine's *Common Sense* and *The Age of Reason*. Paine's writings reinforced Lincoln's natural aversion to animal cruelty.

Thomas Paine (1737–1809) was among the first prominent Americans to advocate for the prevention of cruelty to animals. In 1775, a year before he published his bestselling, revolution-inspiring tract *Common Sense*, Paine published a poem called "Cruelty to Animals Exposed," in which he describes rescuing a kitten that a "crippled wretch" had thrown to a pack of hounds to "see her living mangled limb from limb." In *The Age of Reason* Paine wrote, "Everything of persecution and revenge between man and man, and everything of cruelty to animals is a violation of moral duty. . . . The only idea we can have of serving God is that of contributing to the happiness of the living creation God has made." (Coincidentally, Paine died in the year of Lincoln's birth; their lives overlapped by four months.)

In 1780 the British philosopher Jeremy Bentham, another early proponent of animal welfare, compared the plight of animals to the plight of slaves.

> The day has been, I am sad to say in many places it is not yet past, in which the greater part of the species, under the denomination of slaves, have been treated by the law exactly upon the same footing, as, in England for example, the inferior races of animals are still. . . . What else is it that should trace

the insuperable line? Is it the faculty of reason or perhaps the faculty of discourse? But a full-grown horse or dog, is beyond comparison a more rational, as well as a more conversable animal, than an infant of a day or a week or even a month, old. But suppose the case were otherwise, what would it avail? The question is not, Can they reason? nor, Can they talk? but, Can they suffer?

The New York state legislature passed one of the nation's first anticruelty laws in 1829:

Section 26. MAIMING AND CRUELTY TO ANIMALS. Every person who shall maliciously kill, maim or wound any horse, ox or other cattle, or any sheep, belonging to another, or shall maliciously and cruelly beat or torture any such animal, whether belonging to himself or another, shall, upon conviction, be adjudged guilty of a misdemeanor.

Massachusetts passed a similar law in 1836, but the nascent anticruelty movement was eclipsed by the growing antislavery movement. William J. Schultz, a historian of the humane movement in the United States, wrote that "the crusade against slavery [was] a controversy so all-inclusive that little reforming energy could be spared for a cause which did not obtrude itself upon the public attention."

After the Civil War many abolitionists would turn their attention to animal welfare. The American Society for the Prevention of Cruelty to Animals (ASPCA) was formed in

1866, the year after the war ended. One of its charter members was William Cullen Bryant, the antislavery editor of the *New York Evening Post* and an early supporter of Lincoln.

A century later the anticruelty movement would give birth to a new crusade: the animal rights movement. This shift, according to the philosopher Bernard Rollin, constituted "a major revolution in social concern with animal welfare and moral status of animals." Yet as Lawrence Finsen and Susan Finsen wrote in *The Animal Rights Movement in America*, "there are significant differences between the humane movement and the animal rights movement."

> The humane movement promoted kindness and the elimination of cruelty without challenging the assumption of human superiority or the institutions that reflect that assumption. The animal rights movement, on the other hand, does not seek humane reforms but challenges the assumption of human superiority and demands abolition of institutions it considers exploitive. Rather than asking for a greater (and optional) charity toward animals, the animal rights movement demands justice, equality, fairness, and rights.

In his seminal work on animal rights, *Animal Liberation*, philosopher Peter Singer popularized the term "speciesism" to describe "a prejudice or attitude of bias in favor of the interests of members of one's own species and against those of members of other species." In Singer's words, "All animals are equal"—from ants to humans. Like Jeremy Bentham before him, Singer saw similarities between the treatment of animals and the treatment of human slaves.

Lincoln would undoubtedly be pleased with the progress in animal welfare since his time, though the concept of "animal rights" would mystify him. In some ways, the animal rights movement seems to echo Lincoln's frequent argument regarding slavery: he did not believe whites and blacks were equal in every respect, only that they were born with the same fundamental rights of life, liberty, and the pursuit of happiness. Singer likewise asserts that "the claim to equality [among the races or between the sexes] does not depend on intelligence, moral capacity, physical strength, or similar matters of fact. Equality is a moral idea, not an assertion of fact. There is no logically compelling reason for assuming that a factual difference in ability between two people justifies any difference in the amount of consideration we give to their needs and interests." But Singer takes the argument much further, insisting that "the ethical principle on which human equality rests requires us to extend equal consideration to animals too."

This notion Lincoln would have found a little hard to swallow. For example, Singer advocates a lifestyle that would have been utterly impossible in Lincoln's day. "We should not wear furs," Singer contends. "We should not buy leather products either, since the sale of hides for leather plays a significant role in the profitability of the meat industry." A life without fur and leather in Lincoln's age would have been a difficult life indeed: No shoes, no coats, no gloves, no hats. No harnesses or saddles for horses. No collars for dogs.

Many animal rights advocates have claimed Lincoln as one of their own. Some have even attributed to him these words: "I am in favor of animal rights as well as human rights. That is the way of a whole human being." But Lincoln never said any such thing. The quote is fictitious. While Lincoln passionately advocated kindness toward all living creatures, he certainly did not regard animals as the equals of humans.

IN MARCH 1830, WHEN LINCOLN was twenty-one and still living at home, he helped his family move from Spencer County, in southern Indiana, to Macon County, in central Illinois. With their belongings piled into a crude homemade wagon hitched to a team of oxen, the family slogged through ankle-deep mud and waist-deep water. At least once the wagon was nearly washed away. The journey took two weeks. (Today it takes three hours by car.)

The party consisted of about thirty people, including Lincoln, his father, and his stepmother. Also along was Lincoln's hunting dog. At one point the pioneers crossed a river covered with a thin layer of ice, wading through the freezing water. When they finally reached the other side, a helpless barking could be heard. The little dog had somehow become separated from the rest of the party and was unable to cross the river. The others begged Lincoln to leave the dog behind. Crossing back to fetch it was deemed dangerous and unnecessary. But Lincoln could not resist his poor dog's pitiful cries. Left behind in this wilderness, where bears and wildcats still roamed, the dog would never stand a chance.

So Lincoln waded back across the river to rescue the dog.

"I could not bear to lose my dog," he recalled many years later, "and I jumped out of the waggon [*sic*] and waded waist deep in the ice and water[,] got hold of him and helped out and saved him."

When he reached the animal, Lincoln remembered, the dog made "frantic leaps of joy."

"I guess that I felt about as glad as the dog."

On March 6, 1857, just two days after James Buchanan's inauguration, the Supreme Court rendered a decision that sent shockwaves through the country and steeled Lincoln's political resolve. In a seven-to-two ruling, the high court held that an enslaved man named Dred Scott, whose owner had taken him to live in the free state of Illinois and in the Minnesota Territory, where slavery was also banned, could not sue for his freedom because as a black man he was not a citizen of the United States. In effect the ruling instantly stripped all African Americans, enslaved or free, of any claim to American citizenship.

Chief Justice Roger B. Taney wrote the majority opinion:

The question before us is whether the class of persons described in the plea in abatement compose a portion of this people, and are constituent members of this sovereignty? We think they are not, and that they are not included, and were not intended to be included, under the word "citizens" in the Constitution, and can therefore claim none of the rights and privileges which that instrument provides for and secures to citizens of the United States. On the contrary, they were at that time considered as a subordinate and inferior class of beings who had been subjugated by the dominant race, and, whether emancipated or not, yet remained subject to their authority, and had no rights or privileges but such as those who held the power and the Government might choose to grant them. . . .

They had for more than a century before been regarded as beings of an inferior order, and altogether unfit to associate with the white race either in social or political relations, and so far inferior that they had no rights which the white man was bound to respect, and that the negro might justly and lawfully be reduced to slavery for his benefit.

Lincoln was flabbergasted. The ruling contradicted his core belief: that all men were created equal. Taney, he said, had done "obvious violence to the plain unmistakable language of the Declaration." Now black people had no more rights than a dog like Fido.

In June, Senator Stephen Douglas came to Springfield to give a speech at the statehouse defending the ruling. Nakedly appealing to racism, Douglas declared that "negroes were regarded as an inferior race, who in all ages, and in every part of the globe . . . had shown themselves incapable of self-government." He went on to warn that Republicans favored "the amalgamation between the superior and inferior races." Abraham Lincoln was in the audience.

Lincoln, photographed on February 28, 1857, in Chicago. COURTESY OF
LIBRARY OF CONGRESS

Two weeks later, in his own speech at the statehouse, Lincoln offered what was essentially the Republican response. In calm, reasoned tones, Lincoln explained why he believed the ruling was "erroneous," asserting that it contradicted the wishes of the Founding Fathers:

Chief Justice Taney, in delivering the opinion of the majority of the Court, insists at great length that negroes were no part of the people who made, or for whom was made, the Declaration of Independence, or the Constitution of the United States.

On the contrary, Judge Curtis, in his dissenting opinion, shows that in five of the then thirteen states, to wit, New Hampshire, Massachusetts, New York, New Jersey, and North Carolina, free negroes were voters, and, in proportion to their numbers, had the same part in making the Constitution that the white people had. . . .

In those days, our Declaration of Independence was held sacred by all, and thought to include all; but now, to aid in making the bondage of the negro universal and eternal, it is assailed, and sneered at, and construed, and hawked at, and torn, till, if its framers could rise from their graves, they could not at all recognize it. All the powers of earth seem rapidly combining against him. Mammon is after him; ambition follows, and philosophy follows, and the theology of the day is fast joining the cry. They have him in his prison house; they have searched his person, and left no prying instrument with him. One after another they have closed the heavy iron doors upon him, and now they have him, as it were, bolted in with a lock of a hundred keys, which can never be unlocked without the concurrence of every key; the keys in the hands of a hundred different men, and they scattered to a hundred different and distant places; and they stand musing as to what invention, in all the dominions of mind and matter, can be produced to make the impossibility of his escape more complete than it is.

The speeches were a preview of the Lincoln-Douglas debates to come the following year, when Douglas would be up for reelection. Lincoln spent much of the summer of 1857 laying the groundwork for his bid to unseat Douglas. For Lincoln to win the seat, of course, the Republicans needed to win control of the state legislature, which elected senators.

OWNING A PET DOG REQUIRED considerably more patience and dedication in 1857 than it does today. Much of what pet owners now take for granted was unavailable then: competent veterinary care, vaccinations, packaged food, flea and tick repellents, spaying, neutering. No pet shops are listed in Springfield city directories from the 1850s, although the very beginnings of the modern "pet industry"—it's now estimated that Americans spend at least $50 billion annually on their pets—were already evident.

The most popular pet in the middle of the nineteenth century was the caged songbird. Songbirds make a joyous sound. In a time before recorded music of any kind, these "little dewdrops of celestial melody" (as Thomas Carlyle described them) provided a source of entertainment as well as companionship. On a more practical level, the birds were cheap, plentiful, and relatively easy to care for.

The canary, the most popular songbird, was known as the "universal parlor bird." But many other varieties were popular as well, including cardinals, blue jays, and blackbirds. Some wealthier families owned parrots, which were relatively expensive and sometimes hard to handle. In 1857, while Fido was romping around Springfield with Willie and Tad Lincoln, Edie and Ellen Emerson, the teenage daughters of the poet Ralph Waldo Emerson, were caring for Polly, the family's parrot. In a letter, Ellen described the scene when Polly, whose wings were clipped (common for pet birds at the time), was freed from her cage one day:

> She amused herself by going upstairs like a little child, hanging herself by her beak on the edge of the next stair and then clawing up. Presently Father came down stairs and Polly creaked with dignity to warn him of her presence. Father, looking about, beheld this dear animal patiently coming upstairs, her colours matching the carpet so beautifully that he called to Edie to come and "take away her green cat for no one would see her on the carpet."

A cottage industry developed around bird keeping, and by the 1850s stores selling supplies for pet birds had sprung up in the larger cities. Yet nothing comparable to a modern pet shop would appear until the 1890s. So everything the Lincolns needed for Fido had to be procured independently. A harness maker could easily fashion a collar from scraps of leather lying around his shop. Though Fido does not appear to be wearing a collar in his photos, it's likely he had one,

since a collar was what distinguished an owned dog from a
stray. On the other hand, his fame as the Lincoln dog may
have made a collar unnecessary. And apart from the medicines available through a drugstore like Diller's, Fido's health
care would have consisted of home remedies: a turpentine
bath for the mange, for example.

With their father busy plotting to win a US Senate seat,
Willie and Tad, now six and four, respectively, became Fido's
primary caretakers in the summer of 1857. They relished
the responsibility. The boys were likely in charge of washing
the dog, an especially important task given that their home
had recently undergone a major upgrade. The Lincolns had
added a full second story; fine new carpets had been installed
at Mary's behest, so now she was even less enamored of
Fido's muddy paws. According to the historian Joseph E.
Suppiger, "Lincoln enjoyed watching his younger sons, Willie and Tad, romp through the back yard with Fido while
Robert studied in his room and Mrs. Lincoln sewed and
tatted."

Mostly, though, Fido just tagged along with Willie and
Tad and their friends, a kind of mascot for the neighborhood boys. They included Isaac Diller, the druggist's son,
just a little younger than Tad; Johnny Kaine; and the three
Dubois boys, Fred, Jess, and Link. Henry Remann was probably Willie's best friend, and his sister Josephine sometimes
played with the boys. There was Charlie Melvin, the son of
a local doctor, and of course the Roll boys, Frank and John,
who were almost the exact same age as Willie and Tad. Fido
especially adored the Roll boys. "Fido had always made a fuss
over them," Dorothy Kunhardt wrote, "licking their hands

Willie (standing center) and Tad (seated right), photographed at Mathew Brady's New York studio in 1861 with Lockwood Todd, one of their mother's relatives. COURTESY OF LIBRARY OF CONGRESS

and running halfway home with them when they left after playing with him."

Abraham Lincoln knew all these children well. Their lives were like something straight out of *The Adventures of Tom Sawyer*. There was no shortage of mischief to be gotten into. That summer of 1857 a local paper complained about an increase in "rowdyism" among Springfield's youth: "Yard gates were removed from their hinges in the southern part of the city, leaving the yards open to the depredation of cattle."

There were games to play too. Town ball, a precursor of baseball, was a special favorite. It was played with a solid rubber ball wrapped with yarn and covered in buckskin. The bat was a piece of pine fencing two to three feet long. The children also played blind man's bluff and mumblety-peg, the latter a game in which sharp knives were thrown into the ground—something that would not be permitted on school playgrounds under any circumstances today.

Sometimes Lincoln would join in the children's games to give himself a respite from politics and the law and other adult things. He was said to be excellent at marbles. After supper he would often retire to the parlor with Willie and Tad, lie on the floor, and challenge the boys to keep him from getting up. Eventually he would, with the two boys hanging from him, laughing and squealing. "The dog would be delighted with this lively play," wrote Ruth Painter Randall, "barking and jumping around in great excitement."

For a refreshing break, Willie and Tad and their friends would go to Diller's, where a new soda fountain served cold, flavored soda water, a relatively recent invention. Sometimes, Willie and Tad's father would happen to be there, and he would join the boys for a soda. Of course, Fido came along too. His favorite "duties," according to Randall, included "racing through the house and yard with his young masters and the neighbor children and sharing their play and adventures."

Willie and Tad liked to stage circuses, and Fido was surely a featured performer in these. They taught him to sit, roll over, and fetch. They may have tried to housebreak him too, though this was always difficult with strays. Then

Willie and Tad's bedroom on the second floor of the Lincoln home in Springfield. Fido undoubtedly slept with the boys on their bed many nights. COURTESY OF LINCOLN HOME NATIONAL HISTORIC SITE/NATIONAL PARK SERVICE

as now, there was much debate about the best way to teach puppies to control their bodily functions.

Fido, of course, was not "fixed." While cattle and horses were sometimes castrated, pet dogs would not be routinely spayed or neutered until the 1960s. Thus, controlling the pet population posed a vexing problem. Female dogs in heat were sometimes locked in basements. (This tactic proved less successful with cats.) An 1855 Philadelphia ordinance compelled the destruction of any "bitch in heat" found roaming the city. And when a bitch gave birth to a litter of puppies, even the most tenderhearted owner was inclined to choose the best and drown the rest—literally.

The same was true of cats. When Harriet Beecher Stowe, author of *Uncle Tom's Cabin* and certainly no brute, left her home in Hartford, Connecticut, to winter in Florida in 1876, she informed the renters of her house about her cat's pregnancy: "As to my cat—do you like cats, She has been made quite a pet of—& is going in the way of all the earth to have kittens. . . . The best way would be to have William [the handyman] kill all but one of the kits when they are a day old & then that matter will be disposed of."

Still, cats and dogs reproduced freely. It's possible Fido's doggy descendants are roaming the streets of Springfield even today.

Fido's diet consisted mainly of table scraps and leftovers. He also scavenged for food in the plentiful garbage conveniently strewn about the streets of Springfield. Shop owners simply swept their refuse into the gutters, where it was left to rot. The stench was said to be unbearable in summer.

Commercial dog foods would not be mass produced until after the Civil War, when a British company called Spratt's began selling its dog biscuits in the United States. The company was actually founded by an American, James Spratt, an electrician from Ohio who went to England to sell lightning rods. The story goes that Spratt noticed stray dogs on a Liverpool dock eating leftover hardtack, the rock-hard biscuits that were the staple food of British sailors at sea. Spratt developed a hard biscuit especially for dogs, using a recipe that comprised wheatmeal, vegetables, beetroot, and meat—though Spratt was cagey when it came to identifying the source of the meat. The advertisements intimated it was buffalo.

Spratt's "dog cakes" sold like hotcakes in Britain, where Spratt capitalized on snob appeal and marketed his product to country gentlemen for their hunting dogs. But the American market proved tougher to crack. Frugal Yankees weren't easily convinced to purchase food specially prepared for their dogs, so Spratt launched one of the first major advertising campaigns in US history. Ads for Spratt's dog biscuits were painted on the sides of buildings and plastered on billboards. The company's magazine advertisements boasted that the biscuits contained, "in correct proportion and easily digestible form, every essential food element which the dog constitution requires."

Eventually Spratt's idea caught on. Spratt died in 1880, but his company remained one of America's largest pet food manufacturers until it was bought by General Mills in the 1950s.

FIDO'S PEDIGREE IS UNKNOWN, but this much is certain: he was descended from wolves—as all dogs are. In fact, modern dogs and gray wolves share about 99.9 percent of their DNA. Nobody knows exactly when the first wolves were domesticated. Some experts believe it was more than thirty thousand years ago. How this happened is also a mystery. It may be that, as human hunting techniques evolved, so did our relationship with the precursors of the modern domesticated dog.

In 2014 anthropologists studying a so-called woolly mammoth graveyard in northern Siberia announced something startling. About thirty of these sites, some as small as seventy square yards, are scattered throughout central Europe and northern Asia. Each contains thousands of woolly mammoth bones. The area in northern Siberia, known as Berelekh, is believed to contain the remains of more than 160 woolly mammoths, the giant, hairy ancestors of modern elephants.

How did so many mammoths end up perishing in one spot? Some scientists initially believed they might have been swept up by massive floods or perhaps had fallen through thin ice. But now it's believed the mammoths may have been ambushed by humans, who lived alongside the animals twenty to thirty thousand years ago. And those humans may have been helped by dogs. Among the thousands of mammoth bones at the Berelekh site, scientists have also discovered the skulls of dogs (or, more precisely, their ancestors). It's possible these dogs (or pre-dogs) helped humans corner the mammoths in a convenient spot, perhaps an area surrounded by heavy brush, where the humans could kill the giant animals with arrows. "There's something that's drawing them to that location," wrote Penn State anthropologist Pat Shipman, who led the study. Shipman theorizes that, after the kill, the dogs would have guarded the mammoth carcasses against predators, earning them a piece of the pie, so to speak, and perhaps a warm spot near the fire at night. In the midst of sensible arrangements like this, a bond between dogs and humans began to form, slowly, gradually, over thousands of years.

But there's another, less complicated theory to canine domestication, which David Grimm succinctly summarizes in his book *Citizen Canine*: it just happened. Brave wolves scavenged garbage from human encampments. The bravest wolves scavenged the most and reproduced the most. The space between the wolves and us gradually shrank until, as Grimm puts it, they were eating out of our hands. This is called the theory of self-domestication.

In any event, to convert wild wolves into docile dogs, humans also had to suppress what the German zoologist Helmut Hemmer has called the dog's *Merkwelt*: its perceptual world. This means "whereas a high degree of perception [or alertness], combined with quick reactions to stress are essential for the survival of an animal in the wild, the opposite characteristics of docility, lack of fear and tolerance of stress are the requirements for domestication."

However domestication came to pass, it happened rather quickly (in the grand scheme of things). By about eight thousand years ago, dogs much like those we know today could be found alongside humans wherever they roamed. Eventually these dogs were bred for specific traits, like hunting or herding, leading to the scores of breeds that populate the world today.

Coincidentally, coat color is correlated with temperament in many domesticated animals—those with paler coats tend to be more manageable—and it's believed the earliest domesticated dogs were "tawny-yellow" in color—just like Fido.

But it was still a long way to Fido.

Despite the mutual benefits of their relationship, humans and dogs have not always coexisted peacefully. In fact, the relationship has been surprisingly ambivalent at times. Members of the Yurok Tribe of California, for example, trained their dogs to help them hunt deer. The Yuroks valued their dogs highly for this skill, and when the dogs died, they were given ceremonial burials. Yet the Yuroks banned dogs from their dwellings and forbade naming the animals. They believed that close relationships between humans and dogs threatened the natural order. Zoologist James Serpell put it this way: "Dogs were a potential menace because the critical psychological line that distinguished humans from animals was constantly in danger of being effaced by their presence."

Similar reservations were expressed in medieval Europe. According to the doctrine of dominionism, animals were "lesser beings," meant to be subservient to "more perfect" humans. Thomas Aquinas preached that animals had no souls and were therefore barred from the Kingdom of Heaven. One scholar has called this a "rationalist, anti-animal, Catholic dogma."

In the Middle Ages keeping pets such as dogs or cats was seen as perverted, even heretical. Yet kept they were. "Many of the rituals of pet keeping appear to point to an ambiguous animal–human status," wrote Kathleen Walker-Meikle in *Medieval Pets*. "Pets were given human names, allowed to roam indoors with as much freedom as humans, and rather intriguingly, at their deaths, were greatly mourned over."

What ultimately redeemed dogs was their skill at hunting. Royalty and noblemen, who were somewhat above the reproach of the church, used dogs to hunt for sport, elevating the status of the animals throughout society. Royals also began employing smaller, nonhunting dogs as food tasters and rat catchers—and as simple companions. By the fifteenth century, these "lap dogs" began appearing with hunting dogs in royal portraits, and by the sixteenth century, the dog had been rehabilitated so completely that the English poet Jo+hn Davies celebrated the animal in verse:

> Thou sayest thou art as weary as a dog,
> As angry, sick, and hungry as a dog,
> As dull and melancholy as a dog,
> As lazy, sleepy, idle as a dog,
> But why dost thou compare thee to a dog?
> In that for which all men despise a dog,
> I will compare thee better to a dog,
> Thou art as fair and comely as a dog,
> Thou art as true and honest as a dog,
> Thou art as kind and liberal as a dog,
> Thou art as wise and valiant as a dog.

But even well into the nineteenth century, dogs were still prized mostly for their utilitarian value; they were not true pets in the modern sense. In fact, the word *pet* itself was just beginning to assume its modern usage. The word, which may be derived from *petit*, the French word for small, originally referred to a spoiled child. By the middle of the sixteenth century the term also referred to domesticated animals kept for pleasure, though in writing the preferred term was "favorite."

As late as 1828, when Noah Webster published his *American Dictionary of the English Language*, the meaning of the word *pet* was still fluid. Webster said it could refer to a "lamb brought up by hand," as well as "any little animal fondled and indulged." By 1828 the word had also become a verb: "to treat as a pet; to fondle; to indulge." The word could also be used as a noun to mean a fit of sulking or ill humor (e.g., to be "in a pet").

More recently, there have been attempts to jettison the word *pet* altogether when it comes to referring to domesticated animals. In 2011 the *Journal of Animal Ethics* published an editorial calling for *pet* to be replaced with *companion animal*, and *owner* with *human caregiver*. "Despite its prevalence," the editors wrote, "'pets' is surely a derogatory term with respect to both the animals concerned and their human caregivers." The animal rights group People for the Ethical Treatment of Animals (PETA) refers to pets as *companion animals*, but the ASPCA is sticking with *pets* for now.

After the United States transitioned from subsistence agriculture to large-scale farming and mass production in the 1830s, a new American middle class began to emerge. Until then, even the most coddled dogs were still expected to earn their keep, if only by guarding the house at night. For example, Honey, Lincoln's first dog, helped him hunt. But the new middle class ushered in the first era of true pets, animals kept solely for companionship. In the United States, the history of pet keeping correlates closely with economic advances. The emergence of a new middle class made pet keeping an affordable luxury.

By the 1850s pets were truly becoming part of the family. Owning a dog with no economic purpose was a sign of wealth, an indicator that its owner was a member of America's new bourgeois. In return for food, shelter, and affection, a pet dog reciprocated with something its owner could not buy: status. In effect Fido was a status symbol.

In his groundbreaking 1899 work *The Theory of the Leisure Class*, sociologist Thorstein Veblen decried the "canine monstrosities" that served as status symbols among the wealthy in the United States in the nineteenth century. They were an example of "conspicuous consumption," a term he coined to describe the acquisition of unnecessary luxury goods to display the buyer's wealth.

Dogs continue to be symbols of status, especially in emerging economies. In 2014 the French news agency Agence France-Presse reported that a Chinese businessman paid nearly $2 million for a prized Tibetan mastiff puppy, perhaps the highest price ever paid for a dog. Even in America, some dogs still confer status, from the fancy show dogs that compete in the prestigious Westminster Kennel Club Dog Show to the breeds with aggressive reputations prized in gang culture.

Abraham Lincoln was always embarrassed by the poverty of his childhood. While mentioning his background sometimes served a political purpose, portraying him as a common man—though he was anything but—he usually preferred not to discuss it. Fido was a living, breathing symbol of his success. Perhaps this is another reason Mary Lincoln suffered Fido. She always craved status.

Pet keeping in the United States also correlated closely with social advances. Early humane societies advocated for children as well as animals. In 1877 the Illinois Society for the Prevention of Cruelty to Animals changed its name to the Illinois Humane Society, due to "the large amount of work done for the protection of children."

IN 1857 THE UNITED STATES EXPERIENCED a dramatic economic downturn. The Panic of 1857, as it is now known, was aggravated by the sinking of the SS *Central America*, a side-wheel steamer that went down in a hurricane off the Carolina coast with more than five hundred passengers and crew—and nine tons of gold intended for New York banks. With gold reserves compromised, public confidence in the banks plummeted. (The wreckage was discovered in 1988, and recovery efforts are continuing. So far more than $100 million in gold has been salvaged from the sunken ship.)

As a government town, Springfield weathered the financial crisis better than most communities, though the high cost of living was a constant complaint. According to *The Sangamon Saga*, a history of Springfield and Sangamon County,

> One citizen commented that to house and feed a family of three adults and four children, it would cost $120 a year for rent and an additional $283 for food (meats, $72; flour, $30; tea and coffee, $31; butter, $40; milk, $18; wood, $66; potatoes, $12; sugar, $12; molasses, $2). And the wages of $10.00 weekly had been considered a good pay for a workman the year before.

Lincoln never concerned himself with accumulating wealth, somewhat to Mary's consternation, but as a respected lawyer in the state capital, he enjoyed a healthy income. His record keeping was haphazard, so it's impossible to estimate his annual income in the 1850s, but it likely approached $5,000, a considerable sum at a time when the governor of Illinois earned $1,500 a year.

Still, Lincoln was known for undercharging some clients. When George Floyd of Quincy, Illinois, sent him twenty-five dollars for drawing a deed, Lincoln returned ten dollars to him, explaining in a letter, "You must think I am a high-priced man. You are too liberal with your money. Fifteen dollars is enough for the job. I send you a receipt for fifteen dollars, and return to you a ten-dollar bill."

Occasionally Lincoln came into a windfall. In 1857 he billed one of his most important clients, the Illinois Central Railroad, $5,000 for his services in a single case. The railroad neglected to pay the bill, and Lincoln sued for payment. A jury ultimately awarded Lincoln $4,800. (It's believed this money was crucial to funding his campaign against Stephen Douglas the following year.) Notwithstanding the dispute, the railroad continued to retain Lincoln as its counsel.

The Panic of 1857 seems to have had little impact on Lincoln himself. At the B. H. Luers & Sons shoe store on April 26, he purchased "one pair of gaiter boots at a cost of $12.50 and one pair of kid boots at $1.50"—extravagant purchases at a time when the country was coping with a crippling depression.

4

1858–59

LINCOLN SPENT THE FIRST HALF OF 1858 cultivating support for his run against Douglas. He assembled a team of top-notch advisors, including influential newspaper publisher Norman B. Judd in Chicago and state senator Joseph Gillespie in southern Illinois. "It was Lincoln's special gift not merely to attract such able and dedicated advisers," wrote Lincoln biographer David Herbert Donald, "but to let each of them think that he was Lincoln's closest friend and most trusted counselor."

At the Republican state convention in Springfield on June 16, 1858, delegates unanimously voted for Lincoln as "the first and only choice of the Republicans of Illinois for the United States Senate, as the successor of Stephen A. Douglas." At eight o'clock that night, Lincoln gave his acceptance speech. Paraphrasing Mark 3:25, he said: "A house divided against itself cannot stand."

I believe this government cannot endure, permanently half slave and half free.

I do not expect the Union to be dissolved—I do not expect the house to fall—but I do expect it will cease to be divided. It will become all one thing, or all the other. Either the opponents of slavery, will arrest the further spread of it, and place it where the public mind shall rest in the belief that it is in course of ultimate extinction; or its advocates will push it forward, till it shall become alike lawful in all the States, old as well as new—North as well as South.

Along with the Gettysburg Address and his second inaugural address, this speech stands as one of Lincoln's greatest. The "house divided" metaphor was not a new one; Lincoln himself had used it in 1843 to encourage party unity among the Whigs. But it perfectly illustrated how freedom and slavery were fundamentally incompatible, that they could not coexist within a single nation. Here we see Lincoln's thinking on slavery beginning to evolve, from a policy of containment to a policy of absolutism—the country must be either all free or all slave.

Yet Lincoln would never become an outspoken abolitionist, and abolitionists would continue to regard him with suspicion throughout his presidency. One prominent abolitionist said he was "afraid of 'Abe'" because he was "Southern by birth, Southern in his associations, and Southern, if I mistake not, in his sympathies." Abolitionists were also quick to point out that Lincoln's wife, Mary, came from a slaveholding family. Even the Emancipation Proclamation, which Lincoln considered "the central act of my administration," freed only those slaves in states (or parts of states) "in rebellion against the United States." It had no effect at all on the slaves in the border states still loyal to the Union, namely Delaware, Kentucky, Maryland, and Missouri. And since the federal government had no authority in the rebellious states, the immediate effect of the proclamation was negligible—it freed only a handful of slaves. Secretary of State William Seward, a committed abolitionist, was dismayed by the proclamation, in which, he said, "we show our sympathy with the slaves by emancipating the slaves where we cannot reach them and holding them in bondage where we can set them free."

Toward the end of the House Divided speech, Fido made a brief cameo, in a way. It came by way of another biblical reference, to Ecclesiastes 9:4: "A living dog is better than a dead lion." If not a dead lion, Stephen Douglas was, Lincoln said, "at least a *caged* and *toothless* one."

Lincoln frequently used dog stories as metaphors. In 1848, during his single term as a member of Congress, Lincoln delivered a speech on the floor of the House of Representatives in which he criticized Democrats for continuing to invoke the name of their hero, Andrew Jackson, in that year's presidential campaign, even though the "Hermitage lion" had died three years earlier:

> A fellow once advertised that he had made a discovery by which he could make a new man out of an old one, and have enough of the stuff left to make a little yellow dog. Just such a discovery has General Jackson's popularity been to you. You not only twice made president of him out of it, but you have

had enough of the stuff left, to make presidents of several comparatively small men since; and it is your chief reliance now to make still another.

During the Civil War, in a letter reprimanding a Union officer for using unbecoming language in addressing a fellow officer, Lincoln wrote, "Better give your path to a dog, than be bitten by him in contesting for the right. Even killing the dog would not cure the bite." On another occasion as president, he dismissed critics with the quip, "Dogs will bark at the moon, but I have never heard that the moon stopped on that account."

Lincoln enjoyed poetry; he kept a well-worn volume of Lord Byron's poems in his law office. He was also a bit of a poet himself. "Mr. Lincoln, like many others in their callow days, scribbled verses," his clerk Gibson W. Harris remembered; "and so far as I was capable of judging, their quality was above the average."

In Lincoln's poems, dogs figured prominently as metaphors too. In "The Bear Hunt," which he wrote for a friend in 1846, Lincoln describes "tall fleet" dogs chasing down a bear while a "half-grown pup" and a "short-legged fice" are "yelping far behind." The hunters on horseback shoot the cornered bear, which "spouting blood from every part . . . reels, and sinks, and dies."

> Aforesaid fice, of blustering mood,
> Behind, and quite forgot,
> Just now emerging from the wood,
> Arrives upon the spot.

With grinning teeth, and up-turned hair—
Brim full of spunk and wrath,
He growls, and seizes on dead bear,
And shakes for life and death.

And swells as if his skin would tear,
And growls and shakes again;
And swears, as plain as dog can swear,
That he has won the skin.

Conceited whelp! we laugh at thee—
Nor mind, that now a few
Of pompous, two-legged dogs there be,
Conceited quite as you.

By July Lincoln's senatorial campaign was in high gear, and as his own campaign manager, he was responsible for raising money for the effort. On July 20 he wrote Henry E. Dummer, a client in west central Illinois with an unpaid bill. "I am now in need of money," Lincoln wrote. "Suppose we say the amount shall be $50? . . . Please get the money and send it to me. And while you have pen in hand, tell me what you may know about politics, down your way."

Four days later Lincoln went to Chicago, where he wrote a letter to Stephen Douglas, who was also in the city at the time. Lincoln proposed a series of debates between the two of them. "Will it be agreeable to you to make an arrangement for you and myself to divide time, and address the same audiences during the present canvass?"

This sculpture by John McClarey depicts the Lincoln family circa 1858. Willie is holding his father's hand, Tad is on Lincoln's shoulders, and Fido is at his feet. COURTESY OF LINCOLN HOME NATIONAL HISTORIC SITE/NATIONAL PARK SERVICE

A close-up of Fido in the McClarey sculpture. COURTESY OF LINCOLN HOME NATIONAL HISTORIC SITE/ NATIONAL PARK SERVICE

Four days after that, on July 28, Lincoln and Douglas met for dinner to hash out the details of the debates. The two candidates agreed to seven debates in seven different communities around the state.

The Lincoln-Douglas debates were anticipated as highly as are major sporting events today. A rousing political debate provided a welcome respite from the toil of everyday life. More than ten thousand people flooded Ottawa, Illinois, for the first debate on Saturday, August 21, doubling the town's population. They came by carriage, train, and boat, on horseback and on foot, and stood under a blazing sun in the town square for three hours to watch Lincoln and Douglas exchange verbal blows on a wooden platform erected just for the occasion.

Douglas was known as the Little Giant, for both his political genius and his diminutive stature—at five foot four he was a foot shorter than Lincoln. Supposedly the nickname was bestowed on him by the Mormon leader Joseph Smith, whom Douglas respected. (In 1843 Smith had prophesied that Douglas would run for president.)

As usual, Douglas played the race card with aplomb. If the Republicans were in control, he warned debate audiences, the white race would be mongrelized:

> We are told by Lincoln that he is utterly opposed to the Dred Scott decision, or will not submit to it, for the reason that he says it deprives the Negro of the rights and privileges of citizenship. That is the first and main reason which he assigns for his warfare on the Supreme Court of the United States and its decision. I ask you, are you in favor of conferring upon the Negro the rights and privileges of citizenship? Do you desire to strike out of our state constitution that clause which keeps slaves and free Negroes out of the state, and allow the free Negroes to flow in and cover your prairies with black settlements?

Do you desire to turn this beautiful state into a free Negro colony, in order that when Missouri abolishes slavery she can send 100,000 emancipated slaves into Illinois to become citizens and voters on an equality with yourselves? If you desire Negro citizenship, if you desire to allow them to come into the state and settle with the white man, if you desire them to vote on an equality with yourselves and to make them eligible to office, to serve on juries, and to adjudge your rights, then support Mr. Lincoln and the Black Republican party, who are in favor of the citizenship of the Negro. For one, I am opposed to Negro citizenship in any and every form. I believe this government was made on the white basis. I believe it was made by white men, for the benefit of white men and their posterity forever, and I am in favor of confining citizenship to white men, men of European birth and descent, instead of conferring it upon Negroes, Indians, and other inferior races.

Lincoln's political opponents were known to call him a "nigger lover." While Douglas may not have uttered that term, he clearly implied it. At the fourth debate, on September 18 in Charleston, Illinois, Lincoln answered the charge.

While I was at the hotel today an elderly gentleman called upon me to know whether I was really in favor of producing a perfect equality between the negroes and white people. While I had not proposed

to myself on this occasion to say much on that subject, yet as the question was asked me I thought I
would occupy perhaps five minutes in saying something in regard to it. I will say then that I am not,
nor ever have been in favor of bringing about in any
way the social and political equality of the white
and black races, that I am not nor ever have been
in favor of making voters or jurors of negroes, nor
of qualifying them to hold office, nor to intermarry
with white people; and I will say in addition to this
that there is a physical difference between the white
and black races which I believe will forever forbid
the two races living together on terms of social and
political equality.

Though it grates at modern sensibilities, Lincoln's opinion was widely shared among whites at the time, even abolitionists. Besides, suffrage in Illinois was limited to white
males. Political expediency compelled Lincoln, like Douglas,
to pander to that electorate. Still, Lincoln insisted, even if
they belonged to one of the "inferior races," Negroes were
still endowed with the inalienable rights of life, liberty, and
the pursuit of happiness.

All issues other than slavery were practically ignored in
the Lincoln-Douglas debates, so, really, these two giants of
nineteenth-century politics spent much of their time bicker-
ing over just how inferior Negroes were. Nonetheless, interest in the debates was intense, and not just in Illinois. New
York newspapers sent correspondents to the state to cover
the debates. Reports appeared in papers in every corner of

the country. Abraham Lincoln was becoming a household name.

Election Day—Tuesday, November 2, 1858—was cold and miserable. In Springfield the streets were "in a terrible condition," but voter turnout was the highest ever recorded in the town. Neither Lincoln's nor Douglas's name appeared on the ballot, however. Voters were electing state lawmakers who, in turn, would choose the US senator.

Statewide the Republican legislative candidates actually received more votes than the Democratic candidates, but due to the vagaries of apportionment, the Democrats won more seats.

Though Lincoln lost, his performance in the campaign earned him many accolades, and within days of the election his name was being bandied about as a possible candidate for the 1860 presidential election. In a letter published in the *Cincinnati Gazette* on November 6, Israel Green, who had helped found the Republican Party in Ohio, endorsed Lincoln for president. Two days later, the *Illinois Gazette* in tiny Lacon, Illinois, said Lincoln "should be the standard-bearer of the Republican party for the Presidency in 1860." Soon other papers joined the chorus. The *Olney (Illinois) Times* began running the motto "Abram [*sic*] Lincoln for President for 1860" under its masthead.

The 1858 Senate campaign, like the one four years earlier, left Lincoln in need of cash. "This year I must devote to private business," he wrote a friend in 1859. Unlike after his first Senate campaign, however, Lincoln was not plunged into despair. His campaign had attracted national attention and elevated him to the highest circles of the Republican

Party. In spite of his defeat, the future seemed bright. "Our friends here from different parts of the State, in and out of the Legislature, are united, resolute, and determined," he wrote a friend shortly after Douglas was reelected, "and I think it is almost certain that we shall be far better organized for 1860 than ever before."

But for the time being he would refocus his energies on his law practice and his family.

IN MANY WAYS, 1859 would be the last normal year of Abraham Lincoln's life. He always enjoyed live entertainment, and on Saturday, January 8, he attended a concert by Mrs. J. M. Mozart at Cook's Hall, a new gaslit auditorium in Springfield. Mrs. Mozart, a soprano from Boston, was much admired for her "especially felicitous performances of ballads, an insufficiently heard genre of music," according to one critic. Lincoln must have enjoyed the performance. He was one of fifty-two signatories to a letter published in the *Illinois State Journal* three days after the concert:

> To Mrs. J. M. Mozart,
> The undersigned, wishing to testify their appreciation of your merits as an artist, and their most perfect satisfaction with the concert given by you on last Saturday evening, respectfully request you to give another entertainment, similar in character, on your return from Jacksonville [a town about thirty-five miles west of Springfield].
> Your most excellent treatment of those sterling

songs and ballads, has left a deep and lasting impression on those who had the pleasure of listening to you, and created an earnest desire to hear you once more before you leave the West. Trusting that your engagements will permit you to accede to our request, we are, dear Madam, your most obedient servants.

In response, Mrs. Mozart returned to Cook's Hall that week for an encore performance.

Later that month, Lincoln attended a celebration commemorating the centennial of the birth of the Scottish poet Robert Burns. One newspaper reported that the "supper was splendid and abundant, and was well attended. The toasts offered on this occasion were most appropriate, and were responded to by some of the most talented men of the state, among whom were, Abraham Lincoln . . . and others."

Abe settled back into a familiar routine. His law practice was thriving; 1859 would be a lucrative year, and in a way, the last of the golden years for the Lincoln family. But his love for the legal profession was waning. After the excitement of the Senate campaign, his patience for the trivial lawsuits that comprised the greater part of his practice was running short. Fed up with the demands of a client named Charles Ambos, Lincoln wrote him in June, "I would now very gladly surrender the charge of the case to anyone you would designate, without charging anything for the much trouble I have already had."

At home Lincoln's routine included more than his fair share of chores, something that was much remarked upon by

The Lincolns' front parlor. In this room, visitors to the Lincoln home were likely introduced to Fido. COURTESY OF LINCOLN HOME NATIONAL HISTORIC SITE/NATIONAL PARK SERVICE

his friends and neighbors. Mary had been raised in a wealthy family in Kentucky, with slaves waiting on her hand and foot. She considered domestic chores beneath her. The Lincolns employed an African American maid named Mariah Vance, but so many chores still fell to Abe that one neighbor thought Mary "was quite disposed to make a servant girl" out of him.

On a typical day Abraham would awake before anyone else in the house, perhaps around seven o'clock. If the family cow needed milking, he'd begin with that. The cow was pastured in a field just east of the Lincoln home, and Lincoln had hired some neighbor boys to drive the cow to the home for milking, but on those mornings when the boys forgot, or overslept, Lincoln would go fetch the cow himself, walking through the mist with Fido at his side. A neighbor vividly remembered how Lincoln "fed and milked his own cow," because it was particularly unusual at the time for men from Southern backgrounds to milk cows.

Believe it or not, cow milking was one of those peculiar issues that divided North and South in the years before the Civil War. In New England, men milked cows. In the South, the chore was considered women's work. Was Lincoln's cow milking just another sign that he was "henpecked"? Or was it, as one historian has suggested, a sign of Lincoln's "willingness to adopt 'Yankee' attitudes that some of his neighbors found degrading?" The answer is unknowable, but the fact that the question was plausible demonstrates just how divided the country was.

Still accompanied by Fido, Lincoln would then go shopping. A neighbor recalled that Lincoln "always did his own marketing. . . . I used to see him at the butcher's or the baker's every morning, with his basket on his arm." He would stop at Jim Hall's to buy fresh bread. At the butcher's he would buy meat for breakfast. At the public market he might pick up some fruits and vegetables. In summer the market was notorious for its foul stench. Garbage was strewn everywhere—a feast for Fido.

Returning home from shopping, Lincoln would prepare breakfast for the boys—and Mary, if she was awake yet. A neighbor said Mary required Lincoln "to get up and get the breakfast and then dress the children, after which she would join the family at the table, or lie abed an hour or two longer as she might choose." Breakfast was served in the dining room adjacent to the kitchen, with Fido assuming his usual spot at the table, probably sitting at Lincoln's side, awaiting his share of the meal. Lincoln usually ate a light breakfast: an egg, toast, coffee. After breakfast, he did the dishes.

Then it was off to the office—but only if Mary considered the children properly dressed. "Lincoln would start for his office in the morning," one neighbor remembered, "and she'd go to the door and holler: 'Come back here now and dress those children or they won't be tended today. I'm not breaking my back dressing up those children while you loaf at the office talking politics all the day." At night, Lincoln was also expected to put the children to bed.

Lincoln's law office was on the square, just a short walk from his home. Unless he was scheduled to appear in court, he would spend most of the day in the office, preparing briefs, researching case law, or as Mary suspected, loafing and talking politics. Lincoln was undoubtedly a hard worker—"he would . . . go about the labors of the day with all his might, displaying prodigious industry and capacity for continuous application," Ward Hill Lamon, one of Lincoln's close friends, remembered, perhaps a little too excitedly. But Lincoln also had a tendency to procrastinate. He would tell the same old stories over and over, much to the annoyance of his partner, William Herndon, who did not share Lincoln's sense of humor (or anyone else's for that matter). Lincoln would often read the daily newspapers aloud, another habit that Herndon could not abide. He enjoyed playing chess and checkers with visitors. Sometimes Lincoln would bring "a piece of cheese, or bologna sausage, and a few crackers" to snack on at work. Lincoln "never was a fast worker," Lamon remembered. As a result Lincoln sometimes didn't return home until seven or eight in the evening.

The Lincoln and Herndon law office was far from palatial. One visitor described it as "unkempt, untidy, and uninviting." The furnishings consisted of a small desk, a table, a dilapidated sofa, a rusty stove, a bookcase, and a few wooden chairs. Legend has it that plants grew in the accumulated dirt in the corners of the room.

Lincoln's home was likewise disheveled. Lincoln could wield a mean axe, but he was no handyman. Visitors occasionally remarked on the home's rather ramshackle appearance. According to Illinois congressman William A. Richardson, "His fences were always in need of repair, his gate wanted a hinge, and the scene around the house betrayed a reckless indifference to appearances." Another visitor noted broken panes of glass and broken blinds. Lincoln usually hired John E. Roll to make repairs to the home. In 1849 Roll received "six walnut doors and cash" as payment for work he did for the Lincolns.

On Sundays Lincoln cared for Willie and Tad while Mary attended the First Presbyterian Church; Lincoln himself never formally joined a church. A father looking after his children was considered so out of the ordinary at the time that some of his neighbors took it as another sign that Lincoln was browbeaten.

Lincoln would occasionally take Willie and Tad to the office with him, hauling them in a small wagon. Undoubtedly Fido accompanied them sometimes. At the office the boys would wreak havoc, much to William Herndon's consternation. "The children would proceed to tear up the office," wrote Ruth Painter Randall, "scatter the books and papers, smash the pens, spill the ink, and sometimes as a grand climax heap up books, papers, inkstands, pens, and ashes from the stove in a pile on the floor and then dance on it." Throughout all this, Lincoln was oblivious, lost in his work while Herndon fumed. Lincoln's long-suffering partner said he "wanted to wring the necks of these brats and pitch them out of the windows." But he bit his lip: "Out of respect for Lincoln I kept my mouth shut."

A story in *The Every-Day Life of Abraham Lincoln* vividly illustrates Lincoln's casual parenting style:

> On one occasion Mr. Lincoln was engaged in a game of chess with Judge Treat, when the irrepressible Tad entered the office to bring his father home to supper. As Mr. Lincoln did not obey the summons, Tad attempted one or two offensive movements against the chess-board, but was warded off by the long outstretched arm of his father. When a cessation of the hostilities occurred, Mr. Lincoln, intent upon the game, fell off his guard. It was not long, however, before the table suddenly *bucked*, sending the chess-board and pieces to the floor. Judge Treat was naturally vexed, and strongly urged the infliction of summary punishment upon the miscreant. But Mr. Lincoln only said, as he calmly took his hat to go home: "Considering the position of your pieces, Judge, at the time of the upheaval, I think you had no reason to complain." The Judge,

however, has always said that he never could forgive
Lincoln for not chastising that urchin.

Throughout the week, Lincoln ran errands with Fido
faithfully tagging along. They might stop at Diller's drugstore, where Lincoln would fill a prescription and perhaps
enjoy a flavored soda. And there were daily trips to the post
office to collect his mail. By now Lincoln was much in
demand as a speaker and a correspondent, and a large pile
of letters, neatly wrapped, always awaited him. Fido would
often carry these bundles in his mouth to save his master the
trouble. Lincoln received many invitations to give speeches,
but most he declined. "I regret to say I can not do so now,"
he wrote in response to an invitation to speak in Galesburg,
Illinois, in March 1859. "I must stick to the courts awhile."

ON HIS JAUNTS AROUND SPRINGFIELD with Fido, one of Lincoln's favorite stops was the barbershop owned by his friend
William Florville (or de Fleurville), known universally in
town as Billy the Barber. At this barbershop, Dorothy Kunhardt wrote, Lincoln enjoyed "lounging around long after
his shave and haircut to swap stories with the other men
while Fido waited outside in unhurried communion with
the other animals attending their masters."

A black Caribbean immigrant, William Florville was one
of the most colorful and enigmatic characters in Lincoln's
life. And although he was the black person Lincoln knew
most intimately, he has been all but ignored by most Lincoln
biographers.

This print depicting Lincoln sitting by a fire with Fido at his feet was produced by the Alfred S. Campbell Art Company in 1909, the centennial of Lincoln's birth. The company sold reproductions of the print, which proved quite popular. INDIANA HISTORICAL SOCIETY

It's a surprising omission, especially considering the eventfulness of Florville's own life. He was born in Cap-Haïtien, a city on the northern coast of Haiti, around 1806, shortly after the slave revolt that resulted in the country's independence. During the political turmoil that engulfed the nation after the 1820 suicide of Henri Cristophe, a former slave and self-proclaimed king of Haiti, Florville fled with his godmother to Baltimore, where he was placed in an orphanage and trained to be a barber, a trade that he quickly mastered and, by all accounts, enjoyed. (In the nineteenth century, barbering was one of the few trades open to free black men, and "the business of barbering [was] almost exclusively in the hands of the colored population.")

In the late 1820s Florville moved to New Orleans, where he believed his fluency in French and Creole would be advantageous to pursuing his trade. But as a "free man of color" in the Deep South, he found life disquieting. Unscrupulous slave traders—was there any other kind?—would kidnap free blacks like Florville and sell them into bondage (a scenario depicted in the 2013 film *12 Years a Slave*). So the barber began making his way north, by boat and by foot, carrying his scissors, shears, and razors with him. His destination was Springfield, where he knew a doctor named Elias Merriman, whom he had met as a young man in Baltimore. Late one afternoon in the autumn of 1831, Florville was approaching the village of New Salem, about twenty miles northwest of Springfield, when he encountered a tall, skinny young man walking along the road with an axe slung over one shoulder. It was Abraham Lincoln, who was returning from a hard day's work chopping wood.

At the time Lincoln was twenty-two. Earlier that year, he'd left his father's home for good and settled in New Salem, which, with about a hundred residents, was by far the largest town he'd ever lived in. He would stay in New Salem for the next six years, working a series of jobs to make ends meet:

day laborer, carpenter, boatman, store clerk, soldier, merchant, postmaster, blacksmith, surveyor, lawyer, politician.

When he met up with William Florville on the road to New Salem, Lincoln had recently returned from a trip down the Mississippi to sell a boatload of bacon, wheat, and corn in New Orleans. According to his cousin John Hanks, who accompanied him for at least part of the trip, what Lincoln saw there appalled him. Hanks said he and Lincoln "Saw Negroes Chained—maltreated—whipt & scourged." Hanks reported that Lincoln's "heart bled," that he was "Sad—looked bad—felt bad—was thoughtful & abstracted." It was on this trip, Hanks wrote, that Lincoln "formed his opinions of Slavery; it ran its hot iron in him then & there." Some historians dispute the particulars of Hanks's account, but there is no doubt that in New Orleans Abraham Lincoln witnessed firsthand the horrors of slavery.

In any event, their experiences in New Orleans gave Florville and Lincoln something to chat about as they made their way into town. Both men were gifted storytellers, and they hit it off immediately. When Florville told Lincoln he was short of cash, Lincoln invited him back to his boarding house, where Florville plied his trade for the evening, earning enough money to continue on to Springfield the next morning. Once there, he called on his acquaintance Dr. Merriman, who helped him open a barbershop—the town's first (and, some say, the first in all of Illinois). Soon thereafter he married a woman named Phoebe Rountree, "an attractive mulatto" from Kentucky, with whom he had five children.

Florville quickly established himself as a prominent figure in Springfield. A practicing Roman Catholic, he helped establish the city's first Catholic church, to which he donated generously. He also donated money to help build First Christian Church, which became one of Springfield's largest Protestant churches. His business flourished. By 1835 he had hired an assistant and had started acquiring property throughout the town. (He would accumulate twelve parcels in all.) He was a shrewd speculator too. He purchased four parcels near Illinois Wesleyan University in Bloomington, which he later sold to the expanding university for a hefty profit. And he was an accomplished musician, playing the flute and violin.

In Springfield he certainly stood out—a black, French-speaking, Roman Catholic barber and musician. Fragments of his personality can be gleaned from humorous letters he sent to one of Springfield's local papers, the *Sangamo Journal*.

When he erected a gleaming new barber pole outside his shop in 1833, Billy the Barber assured the *Journal*'s readers that it could withstand "the storms of factions, the hurricanes of the prairies, a common size earthquake, or a runaway team [of horses]."

Two years later he published a letter jokingly beseeching his customers in arrears to pay up: "In conclusion, his majesty would suggest the propriety of his subjects (particularly those whose names are registered) paying into the treasury all demands that may be found against them, as the pecuniary affairs of the government at this time is not in a very flourishing condition."

When he moved into a new shop, he announced the change in another facetious letter to the *Journal*:

The pressure of the times has so embarrassed the people and affected the minds of many, that the

William Florville, also known as Billy the Barber, was Lincoln's confidant for nearly thirty years. ABRAHAM LINCOLN PRESIDENTIAL LIBRARY AND MUSEUM (ALPLM)

razor is not to be trusted in the hands of any but a skillful barber.

The papers tell of men most every day who are in the habit of shaving themselves, who commit suicide with this dangerous instrument. Let every man who is hard run call on Billy and he will take off the beard with such ease that his patron will forget he had the blues. . . .

To the young men who would like the girls to be pleased with them, come and I'll fix you up to take their eye. Old bachelors under the operation of Billy's skill, can be made to look twenty years younger.

It was said that only two men in Springfield truly knew Lincoln: his law partner, William Herndon, and his barber, William Florville. Lincoln was not only Billy's customer; he was also his lawyer. When a clerical error delayed Florville's purchase of the four Bloomington parcels, Lincoln wrote a fellow lawyer there asking for help. "Billy will blame me, if I do not get the thing fixed up this time," Lincoln wrote.

Until he was elected president, Lincoln was clean shaven and one of Billy's most regular customers. In 1859 a haircut cost 25 cents for men, 15 cents for boys, and 20 cents for girls. For shaving Florville charged a flat rate of $1.25 a month. As at Diller's drugstore, Lincoln kept a running tab with the barber, which he paid off annually. Lincoln may have patronized the barbershop as often as several times a week, and on these sojourns he would inevitably have been accompanied by Fido. Occasionally Lincoln would stop by the barbershop at night, when Florville would entertain his customers by playing the flute and violin. It was outside Billy the Barber's that many in Springfield came to know Fido best.

FIDO SPENT A LITTLE LESS TIME with at least one of the Lincoln boys that summer. In early June 1859, Willie, now eight, joined his father on a business trip to Chicago. It was an unforgettable excursion for the boy. From the Tremont Hotel, he wrote a letter to his friend Henry Remann back in Springfield.

> The town is a very beautiful place. Me and father went to two theaters the other night. Me and father have a nice little room to ourselves. We have two little pitcher[s] on a washstand. The smallest one for me the largest one for father. We have two little towels on a top of both pitchers. The smallest one for me, the largest one for father.
>
> We have two little beds in the room. The smallest one for me, the largest one for father.
>
> We have two little wash basin[s]. The smallest one for me, the largest one for father. The weather is very very fine here in this town.

By that autumn Willie was back in school, with Fido accompanying him on the short walk to Miss Corcoran's private academy every morning. (Springfield's public school system was still spotty at the time.) Tad, now six, may have attended Miss Corcoran's as well, though, perhaps embarrassed by his lisp, he was a reluctant student and his early schooling was erratic; when he moved to Washington with the rest of his family less than two years later, he had not yet learned to read or write. (Robert, the eldest son, was away at Phillips Exeter Academy, the famous prep school in New Hampshire.)

In September, Stephen Douglas, burnishing his credentials as a presidential candidate, published a long article in

Harper's magazine entitled "The Dividing Line Between Federal and Local Authority: Popular Sovereignty in the Territories." In the article Douglas rehashed his argument in favor of that "great principle" of popular sovereignty: "The people of every separate political community (dependent Colonies, Provinces, and Territories as well as sovereign States) have an inalienable right to govern themselves in respect to their internal polity." Popular sovereignty, he claimed, could be invoked to block Republican efforts to exclude slavery from the territories; but it could also be invoked to block Southern efforts to impose a national slave code.

The article was Douglas's attempt to maneuver to the middle, to portray himself as a moderate. Lincoln recognized this immediately and sensed the danger it posed to his own possible candidacy. Lincoln knew that Douglas, if he ran for president as many suspected he would, hoped to siphon off Republican votes by appearing to soften his stance on slavery. Notwithstanding his fervent support of "popular sovereignty," Douglas continued to oppose reopening the African slave trade, a position that, in those twisted times, practically made him a liberal in the Democratic Party, especially its Southern wing.

That fall Lincoln embarked on a speaking tour to rebut Douglas. In a series of speeches in Ohio and Indiana, Lincoln mocked what he called Douglas's "gur-reat pur-rinciple" of popular sovereignty, as spelled out in "nineteen mortal pages of *Harper*." Lincoln declared, "Douglas's popular sovereignty, as a matter of principle, simply is, 'If one man would enslave another, neither that other, nor any third man, has a right to object.'" Lincoln also pointed out that slavery was bad for poor whites too: "I say that there is room enough for us all to be free, and that it not only does not wrong the white man that the negro should be free, but it positively wrongs the mass of the white men that the negro should be enslaved; that the mass of white men are really injured by the effect of slave labor in the vicinity of the fields of their own labor."

Lincoln's renown continued to grow, and his name continued to be mentioned seriously as a possible Republican presidential candidate in the following year's election. Publicly, Lincoln deflected questions about his possible candidacy. "I must, in candor, say I do not think myself fit for the Presidency," he wrote the editor of one paper. Privately, however, he was already laying the groundwork for his campaign.

By the end of 1859 it was apparent that Abraham Lincoln would run for president in 1860, and Fido's carefree life would be forever changed.

5

1860–61

IN OCTOBER 1859 Lincoln was invited to give a speech in
New York City the following February. It would be his
Gotham debut, and he prepared his remarks with even more
than his usual thoroughness.

He delivered the speech on February 27, 1860, at Cooper
Institute (now Union), a tuition-free private college that
had been founded by the industrialist Peter Cooper just the
year before. Lincoln spoke inside the school's auditorium,
known as the Great Hall, in the basement of an Italianate
brownstone that still stands at 7 East Seventh Street in Lower
Manhattan. The speech was heavily promoted, and about fifteen hundred people (including a "goodly number of ladies")
paid twenty-five cents each for admission. Wearing a new
black suit that was, according to one observer, "evidently the
work of an unskilled tailor," Lincoln took his place behind
the podium around eight o'clock that night.

"He is rather unsteady in his gait," the *New-York Tribune*
reported the next day, "and there is an involuntary comical
awkwardness which marks his movements while speaking."
His voice, the paper said, "has a frequent tendency to dwin-
dle into a shrill and unpleasant sound" and also betrayed his

backwoods Kentucky roots: he pronounced *chairman* like
"cheerman." He may not have made a good first impression in some superficial respects, but his powerful words
that night would prove that Abraham Lincoln was a brilliant orator, a gifted politician—and a viable presidential
candidate.

For ninety minutes Lincoln held the audience spell-
bound, methodically demolishing Stephen Douglas's argument for popular sovereignty. He pointed out that at least
twenty-one of the thirty-nine signers of the Constitution
explicitly supported federal control of slavery in the territories. "This shows that, in their understanding, no line
dividing local from federal authority, nor anything in the
Constitution, properly forbade Congress to prohibit slavery
in the federal territory; else both their fidelity to correct
principle, and their oath to support the Constitution, would
have constrained them to oppose the prohibition."

The speech was peppered with homespun humor that
delighted the sophisticates in attendance. Speaking rhetor-
ically to Southerners who said they would not abide the
election of a Republican president, Lincoln said:

> In that supposed event, you say, you will destroy
> the Union; and then, you say, the great crime of
> having destroyed it will be upon us! That is cool. A
> highwayman holds a pistol to my ear, and mutters
> through his teeth, "Stand and deliver, or I shall kill
> you, and then you will be a murderer!"
>
> To be sure, what the robber demanded of me—
> my money—was my own; and I had a clear right to

keep it; but it was no more my own than my vote is
my own; and the threat of death to me, to extort my
money, and the threat of destruction to the Union,
to extort my vote, can scarcely be distinguished in
principle.

He ended the speech with a rousing exhortation to
Republicans: "Let us have faith that right makes might;
and in that faith, let us, to the end, dare to do our duty as
we understand it." At that moment, the *Tribune* reported,
Lincoln "bowed, and retired amid the loud and uproarious
applause of his hearers—nearly every man rising sponta-
neously, and cheering with the full power of their lungs."

The speech was printed in its entirety in four New York
newspapers the next day. "Mr. Lincoln is one of Nature's
orators," *Tribune* publisher Horace Greeley gushed, "using
his rare powers solely and effectively to elucidate and to convince, though their inevitable effect is to delight and electrify
as well." The speech led to speaking invitations throughout
the Northeast.

By the time he returned to Springfield in mid-March,
Lincoln had delivered variations of the Cooper Union speech
in Connecticut, New Hampshire, and Rhode Island, cultivating valuable relationships with Republican leaders in
the region and firmly establishing himself as a figure to be
reckoned with on the national political stage. Calls for him
to seek the Republican presidential nomination grew louder
by the day, and Lincoln himself was no longer hesitant about
running. "I will be entirely frank," he wrote a friend in April,
"The taste *is* in my mouth a little."

The Republican National Convention was held in May
in Chicago. Delegates convened in a huge wooden building that had been specially constructed for the event on
Lake Street near the Chicago River. Some said the building, erected in less than two months, resembled a Native
American longhouse, resulting in its nickname: the Wigwam. (Another theory holds that it was simply named after
Tammany Hall's headquarters in New York, which was also
known as the Wigwam.) Lincoln did not attend the convention. He'd wanted to, but at the time it was considered
unseemly for candidates to openly campaign for the nomination; his friends unanimously advised against it. So, instead,
he followed the proceedings by telegraph at the offices of the
Illinois State Journal back in Springfield.

Lincoln's campaign manager at the convention was
David Davis, a three-hundred-pound Kenyon College
graduate with a chin-curtain beard, the kind that Lincoln
would later grow. Davis presided over the Illinois Eighth
Judicial Circuit, where Lincoln practiced. Davis and Lincoln weren't exactly friends—"Lincoln never confided to
me anything," Davis once said—but their shared experiences traveling the circuit from town to town, mile after
mile, year after year, fostered a mutual respect that blos-
somed into a mutually beneficial political relationship.
Davis thought so highly of Lincoln that when he was called
away from the bench for family emergencies, he appointed
Lincoln to replace him, a practice that was not unusual at
the time. Lincoln was so highly thought of by the other
lawyers on the circuit that his rulings were accepted without complaint.

At the convention Davis recruited Lincoln delegates by any means necessary. Many he wooed with promises of plum political positions. Not all these promises would be kept. Many years later, when a friend told Davis it sounded like he "must have prevaricated somewhat" at the convention, the judge reacted with mock indignation. "Prevaricated?" he shouted. "We *lied*—lied like hell!"

Davis also masterminded a scheme to print counterfeit tickets to the convention and distribute them to Lincoln supporters with instructions to arrive early on the day of the nomination. By the time supporters of Lincoln's rivals arrived at the Wigwam, the building was already filled with ten thousand Lincoln stalwarts. (Lincoln would later reward Davis with a seat on the US Supreme Court.)

On May 18, Lincoln won the nomination on the third ballot. The news was wired to him at the *Journal* offices in Springfield. "Well, gentlemen," Lincoln announced, "there is a little woman at our house who is probably more interested in this dispatch than I am."

"Every church bell in Springfield was ringing," wrote Dorothy Kunhardt of that historic day, "cannons boomed, boys exploded fireworks. That evening at the Lincoln home, hurrahing men and women and children passed through the front door into the parlor and out the kitchen way. At this hour Fido usually lay asleep on the floor, but that night there could have been no thought of sleep. There was nothing to do but crawl to the old horsehair sofa and hide under it, trembling the way he did during summer storms."

Later that night a hundred-gun salute rattled every window in town.

The 1860 presidential campaign would be sheer misery for Fido.

LINCOLN WAS JUST ONE of four candidates running for president that year. The Democratic Party, hopelessly divided between hard-line Southerners and more moderate Northerners, split in two. Stephen Douglas was the Northern Democrats' nominee. Vice President John Breckinridge was the Southern Democrats' nominee. And former Tennessee senator John Bell was the nominee of the Constitutional Union Party, a coalition of former Whigs and anti-immigrant Know Nothings. In a four-way race, Lincoln's election seemed assured, but the candidate could leave nothing to chance.

"The morning after the nomination," Kunhardt wrote, "Fido trotted along behind Mr. Lincoln as he walked as usual to market with basket on arm, but the walk was interrupted every few feet by people who made the candidate stop and talk."

Later that day a delegation arrived in Springfield to officially inform Lincoln of his nomination. Willie and Tad were sitting on the front steps when the delegates arrived at the Lincoln home.

"Are you Mr. Lincoln's son?" one of the men asked Willie.

"Yes, sir," nine-year-old Willie answered.

"Then let's shake hands."

At this seven-year-old Tad spoke up: "I'm a Lincoln too!"

Some members of the delegation were surprised when Lincoln did not offer them liquor. "Having kept house sixteen years, and having never held the 'cup' to the lips of my friends then," Lincoln later explained, "my judgment was that I should not, in my new position, change my habit in this respect."

Fido would spend a lot of time under the horsehair sofa until Election Day. There seemed to be a political rally just about every day in Springfield, and celebratory gunshots, fireworks, and cannon fire invariably accompanied each one. A few minutes after Douglas won the Northern Democrats' nomination on June 23, "Hopkins' Artillery was banging out a national salute," wrote Paul M. Angle in *"Here I Have Lived": A History of Lincoln's Springfield.* "Throughout the evening bonfires blazed and rockets flared." Later that summer Springfield Republicans built a replica of the Chicago Wigwam and commissioned a huge cannon, dubbed the

Lincoln at his home in Springfield after a Republican campaign rally on August 8, 1860. Lincoln is the tall figure in white just to the right of the doorway. COURTESY OF LIBRARY OF CONGRESS

Lincoln Cannon, which was fired to summon party members to attend meetings.

Lincoln had always taken comfort in the company of animals, and during that hectic and demanding time, he must have found solace in Fido. The yellow mutt had been the family pet for five years now. Indeed, Willie and Tad could scarcely remember a time when Fido was not part of their family. It pained them all to see Fido so frightened by the seemingly constant barrage of explosions that accompanied the campaign.

The fireworks and cannon fire weren't all that annoyed Fido. The visitors who called on the house at Eighth and Jackson were an additional source of distress. What had once been a steady stream suddenly became a deluge. Lincoln did not personally campaign; again, that was considered distasteful. The office should seek the man, the saying went, and not the other way around. So the campaign came to Springfield. Lincoln bided his time at home, greeting a never-ending stream of guests, great and small. Well-wishers, advisors, and office seekers all came calling. Lincoln would usher each visitor into one of the home's two front parlors. Inevitably, the "Lincoln dog" was one of the attractions of a visit to the Lincoln home.

IN MID-OCTOBER, just a few weeks before the election, Lincoln received a letter from Grace Bedell, an eleven-year-old girl who lived in Westfield, New York. "I have got 4 brothers," she wrote, "and part of them will vote for you any way and if you let your whiskers grow I will try and get the rest of them to vote for you. [Y]ou would look a great deal better for your face is so thin. All the ladies like whiskers and they would tease their husbands to vote for you and then you would be President."

On October 19, Lincoln replied to Grace:

My dear little miss,
Your very agreeable letter of the 15th is received. I regret the necessity of saying I have no daughters. I have three sons—one seventeen, one nine, and one seven, years of age. They, with their mother, constitute my whole family.

As to the whiskers, having never worn any, do you not think people would call it a silly affec[ta]tion if I were to begin it now?
Your very sincere well wisher,
A. Lincoln

On Tuesday, November 6, 1860, Abraham Lincoln was elected the sixteenth president of the United States. The result was not a landslide. With the vote split four ways, Lincoln and his running mate, Maine senator Hannibal Hamlin, won 60 percent of the electoral votes but just 40 percent of the popular vote. Lincoln failed to win even Sangamon County, his home county. In nine Southern states, the Republican candidate's name did not even appear on the ballot, so Lincoln received not a single vote in those states.

The day after his election, Lincoln arose early to go shopping as usual. He went to Jim Hall's accompanied by a black boy. "I am not ashamed to carry a loaf of bread home under my arm," Lincoln told the baker, "but my wife says it is not dignified for a president-elect to carry bread under his arm through the streets, so, hereafter, this boy will come in my place."

A few days later Lincoln went to William Florville's barbershop. Referring to his whiskers, Lincoln supposedly said, "Billy, let's give them a chance to grow." Perhaps it was Florville who suggested the style of beard that Lincoln chose to grow. Unlike a full beard, the chin curtain requires the upper lip to be clean shaven, so Lincoln would still need a barber. In any event, the next time Lincoln posed for a photograph, on November 25, the whiskers on his chin were clearly visible. He would never be photographed clean shaven again.

Beards were just coming into fashion in 1860. For a century, nearly all American men had been clean shaven. Seeing a man with a beard was so unusual that it was often remarked upon. In 1794 a Philadelphia woman considered it worth noting in her diary that she had seen "an elephant and two bearded men" in the street one day. In the 1850s, however, facial hair became trendy, and men started sporting beards of all kinds. In 1857 a Boston newspaper reporter noted that of the 543 men he encountered one day, 338 had full beards. Historian Adam Goodheart wrote that the trend began in Europe:

> American newspapers reported that in Europe, beards were seen as "dangerous" tokens of revolutionary nationalism, claiming that the Austrian and Neapolitan monarchies even went so far as to ban them. In England they were associated with the

sudden burst of martial fervor during the Crimean War. When the trend reached America, connotations of radicalism and militarism traveled with it, spanning the Mason-Dixon Line. It was no accident that the timid Northern Democrats who sympathized with slaveholders—like President James Buchanan—were called "doughfaces." Meanwhile, the Republicans' first standard-bearer, John C. Frémont in 1856, had also been the first bearded presidential candidate in American history.

Lincoln's decision surprised even his oldest friends and led to intense speculation about his motives. "Perhaps it suggested that he was hiding his face because he knew he was not ready to be President," wrote David Herbert Donald in his Lincoln biography.

Or maybe it demonstrated the supreme self-confidence of a man who was willing to risk the inevitable ridicule and unavoidable puns like "Old Abe is . . . puttin' on (h)airs." Or possibly it hinted that the President-elect wanted to present a new face to the public, a more authoritative and elderly bearded visage. Or maybe the beard signified nothing more than the President-elect was bored during the long months of inaction between his nomination and his inauguration.

Another theory asserts that the beard represented a break from the past: the first Republican president would also be the first with a beard. Perhaps the only people who knew the real reason were Lincoln himself and Billy the Barber. In any event, by growing his beard, Lincoln started a trend of his own, one that would last well into the twentieth century. Until Woodrow Wilson broke the streak for good in 1912, the only man elected president without facial hair of some type would be William McKinley.

After the election, the crush of visitors to the Lincoln home only grew. The house was completely unguarded. Strangers seeking political favors from the incoming president merely strolled up the steps and knocked on the front door. They "appeared at his residence," wrote Henry Villard in the *New York Herald*, and "if admission to the Presidential presence be denied them upon the first application they never fail to make a second, third, etc., one, until their wishes are . . . gratified by the object of their obtrusiveness." Villard blamed Lincoln's "inexhaustible good naturedness" for his failure to refuse callers.

Nearly as bothersome was the crush of mail. "That popular mania—the collection of autographs of distinguished men," one newspaper noted, "has proved of late a source of considerable annoyance to Mr. Lincoln also, and hardly a mail reaches here without bringing him numerous requests."

On December 20, 1860, South Carolina left the Union. By the end of January 1861 Mississippi, Florida, Alabama, Georgia, and Louisiana had also seceded. In early February representatives of those six states and Texas met in Montgomery, Alabama, to create the Confederate States of America. As president-elect, Lincoln was powerless to do anything about it. The incumbent, James Buchanan, retained the presidency until March 4, Inauguration Day. Buchanan was a dough-face whose stand on secession was essentially this: it's illegal, but there's nothing we can do about it. While Buchanan dithered, Lincoln chose to remain silent on the impending crisis, fearing any public statements would only make things worse. Many took Lincoln's silence for weakness.

But even with all this on his plate, one question continued to nag at the president-elect: what to do with Fido?

Coincidentally, James Buchanan had faced the same dilemma four years earlier. In fact, from the beginning of the republic, the men who have been elected president have had to figure out what to do with their dogs before assuming the highest office in the land.

George Washington loved dogs. He was an avid breeder of hunting dogs and kept many at his home, Mount Vernon. The names of more than thirty are listed in his journals, including the coonhounds Drunkard, Taster, Tipler, and Tipsy, and the staghounds Sweet Lips, Scentwell, and Vulcan. When he received seven French hounds as a gift from the Marquis de Lafayette, Washington bred them with his own Virginia hounds, creating a new breed that he hoped would be "a superior dog, one that had speed, scent, and brains." (Lafayette's hounds were shipped from France under the watchful eye of a young John Quincy Adams.)

Washington lived most of his two terms as president in Philadelphia, in a large house known as the President's House on what is now Market Street, less than six hundred feet from Independence Hall. Philadelphia was the nation's capital from 1790 to 1800, while a new federal city was under construction in the District of Columbia. (The President's

House in Philadelphia was torn down in 1832, though the foundations of the house and outbuildings were excavated in the 2000s and are visible today.) Washington kept his hunting dogs at Mount Vernon, but the President's House was home to at least one pet dog, Frisk, which belonged to his granddaughter Nelly Custis. Martha Washington also kept a pet parrot in the house.

Washington, however, strictly prohibited his slaves at Mount Vernon from owning dogs. "If any Negro presumes under any pretence whatsoever, to preserve, or bring one into the family, he shall be severely punished and the dog hanged," Washington ordered. "It is not for any good purpose Negroes raise or keep dogs, but to aid them in their night robberies, for it is astonishing to see the command under which their dogs are."

John Adams, who moved into the President's House in 1797 and in 1800 became the first president to reside in the Washington mansion we now call the White House, was also a dog person. It's believed Adams kept several mixed-breed dogs during his presidency. After returning to Massachusetts after his single term ended, his wife, Abigail, wrote one of their granddaughters: "As if you love me proverbially, you must love my dog, you will be glad to learn that Juno yet lives, although like her mistress she is gray with age. She appears to enjoy life and to be grateful for the attention paid her. She wags her tail and announces a visiter [*sic*] whenever one appears." John and Abigail also owned a dog they named Satan for reasons that, unfortunately, have been lost to history.

Thomas Jefferson, on the other hand, was not a dog lover, at least not initially. He complained that they attacked his sheep at Monticello. "I participate in all your hostility to dogs," he once wrote a friend, "and would readily join in any plan of exterminating the whole race. I consider them the most afflicting of all follies for which men tax themselves." Eventually, however, Jefferson came around. While serving as minister to France, he became fascinated with French sheepdogs, a breed known as *chien berger de Brie* (or briard) that dates back to the ninth century. The day before he sailed back to America in 1789, Jefferson purchased a pregnant briard and noted the purchase in his journal: "pd. for a chienne bergere big with pup, 36 Libre [about six dollars], gratuity to the person who brought her, 9 [Libre]." The dog, which Jefferson named Buzzy, gave birth to two pups on the trip home. Buzzy became the progenitor of a new breed of American sheepdogs, and her progeny were well cared for at Monticello. Jefferson described the dogs as "remarkably quiet, faithful, and abounding in the good qualities of the old bitch." Like Washington, however, Jefferson seems to have kept his dogs at his estate while president, though he did keep a mockingbird, named Dick, in the White House.

More recent presidents have kept dogs at the White House; in fact, it's practically become a requirement. According to the Presidential Pet Museum in Glen Allen, Virginia—yes, there is a presidential pet museum—the last completely dog-free administration was William McKinley's, and he left this mortal coil in 1901. Many pet dogs of the presidents have become famous in their own right:

- Laddie Boy, Warren Harding's Airedale, had his own seat at cabinet meetings, as well as his own valet.

- King Tut, a retired police dog owned by Herbert Hoover, was prominently featured in Hoover's 1928 presidential campaign and patrolled the White House grounds at night.
- Fala, Franklin Roosevelt's Scottish terrier, frequently rode with him in the presidential limousine and slept on a blanket in the president's bedroom. He is buried next to FDR.
- Pushinka, a white mutt that was a gift from Nikita Khrushchev to little Caroline Kennedy, was the offspring of a Soviet space dog. She mated with Caroline's Welsh terrier Charlie, producing a litter of four pups: Blackie, Butterfly, Streaker, and White Tips. JFK called the puppies "pupniks."
- Liberty, Gerald Ford's golden retriever, also gave birth to a litter of puppies in the White House. The father was a "champion golden retriever" from a breeder in Oregon.

More recently we've had Rex (Ronald Reagan's Cavalier King Charles spaniel), Millie (George H. W. Bush's English springer spaniel), Buddy (Bill Clinton's Labrador retriever), Barney (George W. Bush's Scottish terrier), and Bo and Sunny (Barack Obama's Portuguese water dogs).

But four years prior to Lincoln's election and the question of what to do with Fido, James Buchanan faced the same decision regarding his own dog, an enormous male Newfoundland named Lara. (Buchanan may have named the dog after Count Lara, the protagonist in Lord Byron's poem *Lara, A Tale*, who returns to Britain after years abroad only to find himself embroiled in political intrigue.) Newfies

Laddie Boy, Warren Harding's Airedale, was famous for attending cabinet meetings and even had his own chair. COURTESY OF LIBRARY OF CONGRESS

are classified as a "giant" dog breed, and Lara fit the bill. He tipped the scales at 170 pounds, easily making him the heaviest presidential pooch ever. In fact, Lara was heavier than seven *presidents*: Madison (122 pounds), Jackson (154), Tyler (160), Pierce (162), W. H. Harrison (162), and Coolidge (166). Immediately before becoming president, Buchanan had served in London as the American minister to Great Britain, from 1853 to 1856. While overseas, he'd had to leave Lara behind at Wheatland, his estate near

Lancaster, Pennsylvania. (Being abroad, Buchanan avoided the political maelstrom that engulfed the country following the passage of the Kansas-Nebraska Act in 1854; he won the Democratic nomination primarily because he'd made fewer enemies than his rivals.)

From London, Buchanan wrote regularly to his niece, Harriet Lane, who was keeping an eye on things back at Wheatland. He was especially concerned about his dog.

"How is Lara?" Buchanan wrote.

Lara was just fine, and after Buchanan won the election in 1856, the Brobdingnagian Newfie received media attention commensurate with his great size. *Frank Leslie's Illustrated Newspaper* sent an illustrator to Wheatland to draw the dog. The paper said the dog was "remarkable for his immense tail and his attachment to his master" and predicted Lara would "become historical as a resident of the White House."

Unlike Lincoln, Buchanan had no reservations about taking his dog to Washington with him. Once in the White House, Lara became a popular attraction—more popular than Buchanan, in many respects. The dog was famous for his peculiar habit of lying motionless for hours, with one eye open and one closed.

For Abraham Lincoln, deciding what to do with his dog was an agonizing choice. Lincoln adored Fido, as did Willie and Tad. But during the campaign he had seen how frightened the dog was of loud noises. The long train ride to Washington alone would terrify the poor creature. And then there was the constant pomp that surrounded the presidency: more twenty-one gun salutes, artillery fire, and fireworks.

Lincoln, whose empathy for animals extended back to the earliest years of his life, realized the White House would be no place for Fido. Sadly, he decided that Fido could not join the family in their new home.

It's also possible that Mary, having put up with the dirty dog for five years, finally put her foot down and insisted he be left behind in Springfield. It was one thing for Fido to muddy the carpets and furniture in the Lincoln home. It was quite another thing to soil the White House. In any event, Lincoln concluded that Fido would be happier in Springfield than in Washington. Reluctantly, Willie and Tad agreed. Once again, his empathy for an animal's predicament stood paramount.

But what to do with the dog? Obviously he would have to be given to a good home. Lincoln thought about Willie and Tad's friends, whom he knew well. "There were so many children Lincoln had romped and talked with over the years," wrote Dorothy Kunhardt. "He had put up rope swings for them, let them sit on his tall shoulders when there was a circus parade, played marbles with them." There was Isaac Diller, whose father owned the drugstore on the town square. Having a druggist as an owner would be good for Fido, since he would have access to the best medicines. Lincoln knew Isaac's father Roland very well; they had spent many hours discussing politics in his pharmacy. And the dog was quite familiar with the drugstore. But Isaac was only six or seven years old—too young to care for the rambunctious dog all by himself.

The more Lincoln thought about it, the more he was convinced that the best home for Fido would be with the

Roll boys, Frank and John. They were, according to Dorothy Kunhardt, "gentle, serious children." Furthermore, their
father, John Eddy Roll, was, along with William Florville,
among Lincoln's oldest friends in Springfield.

Lincoln and Roll had met nearly thirty years earlier,
in the spring of 1831, when Lincoln was twenty-two and
Roll was sixteen. Lincoln had been hired to ship a load of
crops down the Mississippi to New Orleans. But first he had
to build a flatboat. He hired Roll to help him, and in the
month it took to build the boat they began what would be
a lifelong friendship. Afterward Roll apprenticed as a mason
and a plasterer. As soon as his apprenticeship ended, Roll
went into business on his own. He started a construction
company and built more than a hundred houses in Springfield. Later he moved into real estate, buying and selling
buildings and property. In time, he grew quite wealthy.

John E. Roll, his wife, Harriet, and their two boys lived
in a comfortable home on Jackson Street, not far from the
Lincolns. Soon they would move into a far more palatial
residence at Second and Cook, a redbrick Victorian with a
cupola and a large front porch. The Roll home would be a
Springfield landmark until the 1920s, when it was demol-
ished to make way for an apartment building.

The Rolls could give Fido a comfortable, even luxurious
home. They agreed to take him in. The boys, Frank and John
Linden Roll, couldn't have been happier. The latter recalled
many years later:

> My brother and I were about the same age as Willie
> and Tad Lincoln. We knowing an uncle (Charles
> Arnold) living across the street from the Lincoln

This statue of Lincoln and one of his dogs in Fort Wayne, Indiana, was dedicated in 1932. Called *Abraham Lincoln the Hoosier Youth*, the sculpture by Paul Manship depicts Lincoln as he looked when he lived in Indiana (1816–30). The Lincoln National Life Insurance Company commissioned the statue. COURTESY OF KRISTEN GUTHRIE/FORT WAYNE–ALLEN COUNTY CONVENTION AND VISITORS BUREAU home, brought us in close contact with the Lincolns. . . . So we became close friends of the Lincoln boys . . . Willie and Tad and their dog Fido. It was decided inasmuch as the Roll boys were friends of the family we should assume responsibility . . . of his care.

But it was not time for Fido to move in with the Rolls just yet. It was still mid-January, and the Lincolns wouldn't be leaving for a few more weeks. In the meantime, Lincoln was juggling matters of historic importance—how to confront the secessionists?—and more mundane concerns. After all, he had to move his family, including two young boys, halfway across the country to Washington. He withdrew $400 from his account at the Springfield Marine and Fire Insurance Company to finance the trip. (At the time, the government did not pay an incoming president's moving expenses.) This left just $600 in his account. But Lincoln, who was frugal, was far from poor. He later estimated his net worth at this time to be around $15,000, including cash, property, stocks, bonds, and debts he was owed. (His presidential salary was $25,000 annually. That's more than $500,000 in today's money, so the president's salary has not quite kept up with inflation—currently it's $400,000. But the perks are now much better.)

The Lincolns also sold off most of their home furnishings, placing an ad in the *Illinois State Journal* to announce the sale:

AT PRIVATE SALE—THE FURNITURE CONSISTING OF Parlor and Chamber Sets, Carpets, Sofas, Chairs,

Wardrobes, Bureaus, Bedsteads, Stoves, China, Queensware, Glass, etc. etc., at the residence on the corner of Eighth and Jackson streets is offered at private sale without reserve. For particulars apply on the premises at once.

One piece of furniture that was not sold off was Fido's favorite horsehair sofa.

John E. Roll bought many of Lincoln's furnishings, but perhaps Lincoln's best customer was his friend Samuel H. Melvin. As was his wont, Lincoln carefully wrote out a receipt for Melvin's purchase:

6 Chairs 2.00 12.00
1 Spring Mattress 26.00
1 Wardrobe 20.00
1 Whatnot 10.00
1 Stand 1.50
9 1/2 yds. Stair Carpet .50 [per yd.] 4.75
4 Comforters 2.00 8.00

$82.25
Recd payment
Springfield
A. LINCOLN

Many of the items purchased from the Lincoln home would become treasured heirlooms for generations in their new families.

Lincoln also sold off his two horses, Tom and Old Bob. Tom's new owner is unknown, but Old Bob, Lincoln's favorite mount, was sold to an Irish drayman named John Flynn, who planned to use the horse to pull one of his flat-bed delivery carts.

Lincoln then arranged for the house to be rented to a railroad executive, Lucian Tilton, and his wife for $350 a year. William Florville (Billy the Barber) agreed to keep an eye on the property while Lincoln was away. Lincoln also took out an insurance policy on the house for $24 a year. (The property was valued at $3,000.)

The Lincolns also threw out or destroyed numerous family photographs and letters, depriving—wittingly or unwittingly—future generations of some of the more intimate details of their lives.

Some Lincoln scholars have claimed that the Fido photographs were taken around this time, while final preparations were being made for the family's departure from Springfield. Legend has it that Willie and Tad took Fido to a photographic studio on the square and had the mutt sit for the photos so they could have a remembrance of their dear pet.

In her 1955 book *Lincoln's Sons*, Ruth Painter Randall wrote that "in the first few weeks of 1861 . . . a Springfield photographer took the pictures, Fido looking very patient and as if anxious to do what was required in this strange performance." More recently, Harold Holzer wrote, "If the boys could not take their pet to the White House, at least they would have as a keepsake their own photograph of the dog they were forced to leave behind." However, Holzer has also acknowledged, "It is impossible to know for certain whether [the photos were] taken before the Lincolns left Springfield, or after the assassination."

It was certainly not unusual at the time for a well-to-do family to photograph a pet—it was another sign of status to which Lincoln and his wife would not have objected. As soon as the technology became widely available in the 1840s, pet dogs were a favorite subject of studio photographers.

The Lincoln family's photo collection included a tattered photograph of Fido, but its provenance is uncertain. The boys may have taken it to Washington—or it may have been added to the collection later. The latter seems more likely. The surviving copies of the Fido photographs are marked on the back:

F. W. INGMIRE,
PHOTOGRAPHIC ARTIST,
City Gallery,
West Side of Public Square,
SPRINGFIELD, ILL.

Frederick W. Ingmire was an interesting character in his own right, a Baptist minister from Albany, New York, who moved to Springfield around 1859. With six children, Ingmire was always in need of extra cash and worked many side jobs. For a time he sold insurance, then typewriters.

In 2014 James Cornelius, the curator of the Abraham Lincoln Collection at the Abraham Lincoln Presidential Library and Museum, wrote:

> In 1860–61 Rev. Ingmire was working as a Baptist minister and a sewing-machine agent. He ran dozens of ads in those years for his agency. He

began to pay for a photographer's license ($10.00 during wartime) in 1862. And he first ran an ad for that new business in October 1864, when lots of soldiers passing through Camp Butler [a Union Army camp near Springfield] made it a profitable trade.

Although these facts do not prove that Ingmire did not snap Fido in 1860–61, it seems to make it very unlikely.

There is also no evidence that Lincoln and Ingmire were anything more than passing acquaintances, though Ingmire's eldest daughter, Mary, would later claim she once held Lincoln's hand when she was a little girl. The 1860–61 Springfield directory lists three photographers, none of whom is Ingmire, and each of whom was much more likely than Ingmire to have taken the Fido photos before the Lincolns left Springfield. It's likely Ingmire had begun to dabble in photography by early 1861, but why would Lincoln entrust a hobbyist to take the pictures when professional photographers were readily available?

It's more likely the photographs were taken shortly after Lincoln's assassination. Ingmire, who struggled with a "disposition of melancholy," died after overdosing on morphine in 1876. He was fifty-three. According to his obituary in the *Illinois State Journal*, "His failure to accumulate a competence in his growing age, and the necessity to still labor, so weighed upon him as to produce a degree of mental aberration which is so often accompanied by the taking of opiates."

On the evening of Wednesday, February 6, while the seceding states were meeting in Alabama to form their own more perfect union, Abraham and Mary Lincoln hosted a final farewell reception at their home in Springfield. Some seven hundred people were in attendance. It's said the crowd was so thick that it took twenty minutes to walk across the parlor. Fido was probably camped out upstairs on Willie and Tad's bed.

That next night, Abraham, Mary, Willie, and Tad Lincoln slept in their home for the last time. In all likelihood this was also Fido's last night in the house. With most of their belongings now either sold or in storage, the next day, Friday, February 8, the family moved into a suite at the Chenery House, where the going rate was two dollars a day.

Presumably, that's also the day that Fido moved in with his new family. "Fido may have wondered that day why Willie and Tad hugged and petted him so much more than usual, and why they were crying," wrote Ruth Painter Randall. "The only thing a dog could do was lick their faces to show he was sorry they felt so bad."

Lincoln also gave the Rolls Fido's favorite piece of furniture: the seven-foot-long horsehair sofa where he liked to nap and where he sought refuge in times of stress. "This familiar landmark," Dorothy Kunhardt wrote, "was a piece of his old life coming with him into the new." The Rolls were also given some rules for caring for Fido, which one of the boys, John Linden Roll, explained to Kunhardt many years later:

The Roll boys had been given explicit instructions

for Fido's care. They had promised never to leave him tied up in the backyard by himself. He was not to be scolded for wet or muddy paws. He was to be allowed inside whenever he scratched at the door and be allowed in the dining room at dinner time because he was used to being given tastes by everybody around the table.

All of these rules the Rolls readily agreed to. They were delighted to welcome Fido into their home.

On Sunday, February 10, the day before his departure, Lincoln visited his law office one last time. Sitting down with his partner, William Herndon, Lincoln went over the firm's outstanding cases. Then, according to Herndon, Lincoln stretched himself out on the old sofa in the office and lay there "for some moments, his face towards the ceiling."

"Billy," Lincoln asked after a long silence, "how long have we been together?"

"Over sixteen years," Herndon answered.

"We've never had a cross word during all that time, have we?"

"No, indeed we have not."

Lincoln got up and gathered his things. Herndon accompanied him down the stairs. Pointing up at the firm's signboard, which "swung on its rusty hinges at the foot of the stairway," Lincoln told his partner, "Let it hang there undisturbed. Give our clients to understand that the election of a president makes no change in the firm of Lincoln and Herndon. If I live I'm coming back some time, and then we'll go right on practicing law as if nothing had ever happened."

Lincoln was melancholy. He told Herndon he was convinced he would never return to Springfield alive. Herndon told him to banish such thoughts, that it was not in keeping with "the proper ideal of a president."

"But," Lincoln replied, "it is in keeping with my philosophy."

The next morning broke cold and rainy. It was Monday, February 11, 1861—the day before his fifty-second birthday. Lincoln arose early and rode a carriage to Springfield's dingy Great Western Railroad depot to board the special train that would carry him to Washington. (Mary, Willie, and Tad would leave later that day, catching up with Lincoln the next morning in Indianapolis.) The trunks containing the family's belongings were loaded onto the train. Lincoln had labeled them himself: A. LINCOLN, THE WHITE HOUSE, WASHINGTON D.C.

About a thousand people had gathered to see Lincoln off. Certainly John E. Roll and his two boys were there to say good-bye, and surely they brought Fido along to say good-bye, too.

Lincoln's "breast heaved with emotion," according to one onlooker. A few minutes before eight o'clock, he climbed the steps up to the platform at the rear of the train and addressed his friends and neighbors for what he feared might be the final time.

> My friends—No one, not in my situation, can appreciate my feeling of sadness at this parting. To this place, and the kindness of these people, I owe everything. Here I have lived a quarter of a century,

and have passed from a young to an old man. Here my children have been born, and one is buried. I now leave, not knowing when, or whether ever, I may return, with a task before me greater than that which rested upon Washington. Without the assistance of that Divine Being, who ever attended him, I cannot succeed. With that assistance I cannot fail. Trusting in Him, who can go with me, and remain with you and be everywhere for good, let us confidently hope that all will yet be well. To His care commending you, as I hope in your prayers you will commend me, I bid you an affectionate farewell.

6

1861–66

With his master now in the White House, Fido's fame began to grow well beyond Springfield. Strangers from far and wide came to visit the new president's hometown, and many took the time to seek out the chief executive's "old yaller dog." Fido gave each of them his customary greeting, "depositing his muddy yellow fore paws plump on the breast." What had once been an annoyance was now an unusual presidential souvenir. Some visitors probably even plucked a few hairs from the put-upon pooch's yellow coat as a keepsake.

Fido, of course, could not understand the reason for this special attention, though he suffered it with his usual grace. His life with the Roll family was as ideal as his life with the Lincolns had been. He must have missed his old family, especially Willie and Tad, but their absence was mitigated by the unbridled bliss a pampered pet enjoys. New adventures still awaited him every day in Springfield, new games of town ball and tag, blind man's bluff and mumblety-peg. Fido continued to romp around town at will, frequenting Diller's and Billy the Barber's. Willie and Tad were gone, but

John Linden Roll, photographed on June 25, 1943, his eighty-ninth birthday. Roll and his brother Frank looked after Fido after the Lincolns moved to Washington. ABRAHAM LINCOLN PRESIDENTIAL LIBRARY AND MUSEUM (ALPLM)

the Roll boys, Frank and John, were excellent substitutes. And his other old friends were still around: Isaac Diller and the Dubois boys, Fred, Jess, and Link.

"We had our chores to do," John Linden Roll recalled many years later, "and he liked to visit around the neighborhood, he was a friendly dog."

The Civil War began. Fido and his friends grew older.

But Fido never truly forgot his first master.

THE WHITE HOUSE, meanwhile, became as animal friendly as the light brown house in Springfield had been. When the

public learned of Willie and Tad's love of animals, unsolic-
ited (and, to Mary at least, unwanted) pets began appearing
at the mansion—kittens, rabbits, goats, and ponies. The boys
loved them all, especially the goats. They named one Nanko
and taught him to pull a cart. The other goat, Nanny, was
notorious for destroying the flower beds.

Lincoln was very fond of the goats as well. He enjoyed
watching them frolic on the lawn. One day, Nanny disap-
peared. "'Nanny Goat' is lost," Lincoln wrote to Mary, who
was traveling at the time. "Mrs. Cuthbert [the housekeeper]
& I are in distress about it." Nothing more is known about
Nanny. Maybe the gardener did it.

There was even a new dog. His name was Jip (or Gyp).
One visitor to the White House remembered Jip as a "very
beautiful little dog" who "barks & stands straight up on his
hind feet & holds his fore feet up." All in all, Jip was said to
be "a very cunning little fellow."

Ruth Painter Randall, biographer of the Lincoln sons,
believed this parade of new animals "quickly crowded out"
any "regrets over Fido [being] left at Springfield," but that
seems unlikely. If Willie and Tad had taken a photograph
of Fido with them to the White House, how could they
not have gazed upon it occasionally, remembering their old
yellow friend back in Springfield? Even if they hadn't, how
could they ever have forgotten their faithful companion?

As the war dragged on, Lincoln seemed to take ever-
greater comfort in the company of animals. He was delighted
when Jip would join him for lunch, standing on his hind
legs, begging for scraps he never failed to receive.

Cats also continued to give him great comfort, as an
old friend from Springfield named N. W. Miner learned

when he visited the White House. Many years later, Miner's daughter, Mary Miner Hill, recalled the incident:

> My father saw by the president's place an extra chair and also an extra fork. The door opened and in walked a beautiful tabby cat and jumped in the chair next to the President. Mrs. Lincoln said to my father: "Mr. Miner, don't you think it is shameful for Mr. Lincoln to feed tabby with a gold fork?" Mr. Lincoln replied: "Mr. Miner, if the gold fork was good enough for Buchanan I think it is good enough for Tabby," and he fed the cat during the meal.

Once, while visiting Union troops at City Point, Virginia, Lincoln noticed three tiny kittens on the floor of the telegrapher's tent, "crawling about . . . and mewing pitifully." The president inquired as to the mother cat's whereabouts. Informed that she had died, Lincoln gently picked up the three kittens, sat down, and put them on his lap. As he stroked them he softly said, "Poor little creatures! Don't cry! You'll be taken care of." He ordered one of the officers to see that the kittens were well cared for. Before leaving, he returned to the tent three more times to check in on the kittens and to play with them.

IN EARLY FEBRUARY 1862, a little more than a month after his eleventh birthday, Willie Lincoln became very sick. He had a fever and became delirious. The precise cause of his illness is hard to know; Lincoln biographer Michael

Burlingame speculates that it might have been typhoid, smallpox, or tuberculosis. "Some suspected that the White House basement promoted disease," wrote Burlingame. William O. Stoddard, one of Lincoln's private secretaries, remembered that the basement was "perennially overrun with rats, mildew, and foul smells" and likely contributed to Willie's illness.

As the days went by, Willie's condition worsened. He died on February 20. His parents, of course, were utterly distraught. "My poor boy," wrote Lincoln. "He was too good for this earth. God has called him home. I know that he is much better off in heaven, but then we loved him so. It is hard, hard to have him die!" Mary Lincoln was so overcome with grief that some feared for her sanity. It was said that Tad cried almost nonstop for a full month after his beloved older brother and best friend passed away. (Tad himself would die, probably of pleurisy, at eighteen. Of Lincoln's four sons, only Bob would survive past young adulthood, dying at eighty-two in 1926.)

In 1863 William Florville, Springfield's famous Billy the Barber, wrote a long letter to his old friend and longtime customer. In it he expressed hope for a quick peace and concern for Lincoln's health. He thanked Lincoln for issuing the Emancipation Proclamation earlier that year: "I and my people feel greatful to you for it. The Shackels have fallen, and Bondmen have become freemen to Some extent already under your Proclamation."

Florville went on:

I was sorry to hear of the death of your son Willy.

I thought him a Smart lad for his age, so Consider-
ate, so Manly; his Knowledge and good Sence, far
exceeding Most boys far advanced in years yet the
time comes to all, all must die. . . . Tell Taddy that
his (and Willys) Dog is alive and Kicking doing well
as he stays Mostly at John E. Rolls with his Boys.

Since Florville wrote that the dog stayed "mostly" with
the Rolls, it seems that, by 1863, more than two years after
the Lincolns had left Springfield, Fido had become a kind
of community property in the town, cared for and loved by
more than one family. Clearly the dog was a local treasure.

In the letter, Florville also updated Lincoln on his property, just as he'd promised: "Your residence here is kept in
good order. Mr. Tilton has no children to ruin things."

EVEN SEVENTY-FIVE YEARS LATER, Isaac Diller vividly remembered the morning of April 15, 1865. In 1940 he described
to Dorothy Kunhardt how his family "was sitting down to
breakfast when they got the word that Mr. Lincoln had been
assassinated the night before." They all began to cry.

On May 3, 1865, Abraham Lincoln, who had wondered
whether he would ever return to Springfield, did return. So
did Willie. Two coffins arrived that day—the smaller one for
Willie, the larger one for his father. The Lincoln home was
draped all around in black bunting. The Tiltons, who were
still renting the house, opened it to the mourners who had
flocked to Springfield. Mrs. Tilton later estimated that they
came at the rate of two hundred every five minutes.

Lincoln's hearse in Springfield. COURTESY OF LIBRARY OF CONGRESS

Little John Roll took Fido to the Lincoln home that day so the dog could greet the mourners. It was probably the first time Fido had been back inside the house since he'd moved in with the Roll family a little more than four years earlier. In *Twenty Days*, their account of the nation's mourning after the Lincoln assassination, Dorothy Kunhardt and her son Philip B. Kunhardt Jr. wrote:

> On the sad day that young John Roll brought Fido back to meet the hundreds of out-of-town visitors, the little wagging-tailed dog was in high spirits. "The Lincoln Dog" caught everyone's fancy immediately as being an important historical character.

John Flynn brought Lincoln's old horse Old Bob back to the Lincoln home that day too. Now sixteen and nearing the end of his life, his belly more round than when Lincoln had left Springfield, the horse was probably tired, but he suffered the attention stoically.

According to the Kunhardts, "Two of the greatest attractions at the Lincoln house on May the third" were Fido and Old Bob. They were petted and prodded. Old Bob had to be protected from visitors eager to pluck hairs from his tail. No doubt Fido lost some fur to souvenir hunters that day. Lincoln's assassination had transformed Fido and Old Bob into living, breathing relics of the fallen president.

There were reports that two speculators offered John Flynn $500 for Old Bob, a fantastic sum for a sixteen-year-old workhorse. The buyers planned to take Old Bob on tour and charge people for the privilege of seeing the famous Lincoln horse with their own eyes. Apparently the plan fell through. No evidence has ever been found to prove the horse was ever put on public display—no handbills, no broadsides, no advertisements. It seems Old Bob stayed with John Flynn, though the ultimate fate of the horse remains a mystery.

The next day, May 4, a long, mournful parade wound its way through Springfield to the burial site at Oak Ridge, a quiet cemetery about two miles from the center of town. Old Bob, draped in a black mourning blanket, walked right behind the hearse, riderless. His reins were held by the Reverend Henry Brown, an African American preacher who had occasionally done odd jobs for the Lincolns. Exactly a month earlier, on April 4, Old Bob had marched in a parade celebrating the fall of Richmond, the Confederate capital. On that day he had been draped in a red, white, and blue blanket.

Lincoln's faithful horse, Old Bob, draped in a black mourning blanket for the president's funeral procession in Springfield on May 4, 1865. Holding the reins is the Reverend Henry Brown. COURTESY OF LIBRARY OF CONGRESS

William Florville—Billy the Barber—was invited to walk with a coterie of Lincoln's closest friends from Springfield, near the front of the parade. Instead he chose to walk with the "colored" contingent at the very end of the procession. He said he wanted to be with "those who cared most" about the dead president. Mary Lincoln was too distraught to attend. She had stayed behind at the White House with twelve-year-old Tad. Robert Lincoln, now twenty-one, represented the family at the funeral.

It's said that Fido was there too, watching the slow funeral procession "forlornly," mutely wishing farewell to his old master and his young friend, both dead too soon.

IT'S NOW WIDELY BELIEVED among Lincoln researchers that the Fido photographs, rather than being taken before the

Lincolns left for Washington in early 1861, were actually taken around the time of the funeral in Springfield. John Eddy Roll, Lincoln's friend and the father of the two Roll boys, sensing Fido's historical importance—and, perhaps, a financial opportunity—took the dog to F. W. Ingmire's studio. Roll was certainly not afraid to capitalize on his relationship with Lincoln. For the rest of his life he would peddle Lincoln relics, including pieces of the walnut doors he was given for making repairs to the Lincoln home. It's believed Roll had the photographs reproduced and then sold them as souvenirs, which became quite popular.

After the assassination, wrote historian Harold Holzer, "portraits of the dog—along with images of everything else Lincoln knew and touched—were widely published and sold to an eager public." Fido became a treasured part of the parlor albums in countless American homes. Tad may have acquired one of these images of his old yellow dog, which would explain how a Fido photo ended up in the Lincoln family's collection.

In 1893 John Eddy Roll copyrighted one of the images and turned it into a *carte de visite* that was sold at the World's Columbian Exposition held in Chicago that year. These were apparently popular souvenirs, proving Fido's fame endured long after Lincoln was president. (A Fido CDV now, um, fetches more than $3,000.)

CHARLES PLANCK WOULD HAVE BEEN lost to history—and rightfully so—if not for an event that occurred sometime in 1866, the year after Lincoln was assassinated. Planck was a ne'er-do-well; today we would call him a loser. He was twenty-four years old in 1866, but he had not accomplished much of anything in life. According to the Springfield city directory, he was working as a clerk at his brother's confectionery. One Springfield resident remembered that Planck was "somewhat given to intoxicating beverage"—in other words, he was a drunk. Charlie Planck, clearly unhappy with his station in life, was also prone to fits of anger.

So there he was, one day in 1866, heavily intoxicated, sitting on a curb, head hanging down. Some accounts say he was whittling a stick. In any event, he was holding a "sharp, long bladed knife." A friendly yellow dog came up to him, the way it often approached strangers. And it put its muddy forepaws on Charlie Planck. In a blind, drunken rage, Planck drew the knife and plunged it into Fido's chest.

Wounded and whimpering, the most famous dog in Springfield—and in all of America, for that matter—struggled to make his way back home, back to the Roll house, hobbling, hobbling, while blood poured from his chest. But it was too far. He could make it only as far as the Universalist church on the corner of Fifth and Cook, just three blocks from the Roll mansion.

Fido, mortally wounded, his yellow coat matted with blood, labored to the back side of the church.

He curled up tight against the chimney, as if to keep warm.

And there he died.

PLANCK WAS NEVER CHARGED with a crime; after all, killing a dog, even a famous one, was hardly a capital offense at the time. In 1868 he would be arrested for shooting and

wounding a man during an argument. After this, Charlie
Planck slithered back into the obscurity he so richly deserved.

It was several days before Fido's body was discovered
behind the church. The two Roll boys buried Abraham Lincoln's faithful canine companion in their backyard.

In 1964 a Springfield resident named Lenora Smith published a small pamphlet called *The Legend of Fido*. It was
based on her father's conversations with an unnamed "fine
old gentleman" who had taken care of Fido as a little boy—
presumably John Linden Roll. "Then one fine morning old
yaller dog wandered away," Roll supposedly told Smith's
father, "in search of adventure, I guess—or a tasty meal,
maybe. That was the last time we saw him alive." Roll said
he and his brother found Fido behind the church, "where he
had laid down to die. We carried him home and buried him.
We covered his grave with flowers. He was just a common
cur. Just an old yaller dog."

John Linden Roll also recalled Fido's demise in a letter
to Dorothy Kunhardt that Roll composed in a shaky hand
shortly before his own death at age eighty-nine in 1943:

> We possessed the dog for a number of years when
> one day the dog, in a playful manner put his dirty
> paws upon a drunken man sitting on the street
> curbing [who] in his drunken rage, thrust a knife
> into the body of poor old Fido. He was buried by
> loving hands. So, Fido, just a poor yellow dog, met
> the fate of his illustrious master—Assassination.

ACKNOWLEDGMENTS

There is so much we will never know about the yellow mutt that Abraham Lincoln adopted in 1855. At the time, pets lived their lives almost entirely outside the historical record. Due to the fame of his owner, however, Fido's life was better documented than that of practically any other pet in the mid-nineteenth century. By combining these bits and pieces—fleeting mentions in newspapers and correspondence, the recollections of friends and neighbors, those three tattered photographs—with the well-documented stories of Lincoln's affection for animals of all kinds, along with what we know of the status and lives of pets generally in antebellum America, I have, I hope, been able to reconstruct Fido's life, however imperfectly.

Some sources proved indispensable. For general biographical information about Lincoln, I relied heavily on *Lincoln* by David Herbert Donald and *Abraham Lincoln: A Life* by Michael Burlingame. Both works are essential to understanding and appreciating Lincoln.

For researching the history of pets and the domestication of dogs, Katherine C. Grier's *Pets in America: A History* was essential, as was *The Domestic Dog: Its Evolution, Behaviour and Interactions with People*, edited by James Serpell.

It practically goes without saying that, without Dorothy Kunhardt's dogged research, this work would not have been possible. (Forgive the pun; I think Dorothy would have appreciated it.) She managed to track down two of Fido's last living companions, Isaac Diller and John Linden Roll. Without their recollections, Fido's story might have been lost forever.

Ruth Painter Randall has long been overshadowed by her more famous husband, the noted Lincoln scholar James G. Randall. Yet she was a formidable Lincoln scholar in her own right, exploring otherwise overlooked aspects of the president's life. Her books *Lincoln's Animal Friends* and *Lincoln's Sons* were never far from my side while I was researching and writing this book.

My research was also abetted by that modern wonder, the Internet. The following two websites were invaluable:

- The Lincoln Log (www.thelincolnlog.org), a daily chronology of Lincoln's life, curated by the Papers of Abraham Lincoln, a project of the Illinois Historic Preservation Agency and the Abraham Lincoln Presidential Library and Museum.
- The Collected Works of Abraham Lincoln (http://quod.lib.umich.edu/l/lincoln/), a searchable database of all Lincoln's correspondence, speeches, and other writings, maintained by the Abraham Lincoln Association in Springfield.

The website of the Presidential Pet Museum in Glen Allen, Virginia, (http://presidentialpetmuseum.com) was helpful too.

Of course numerous individuals and institutions also helped make this work possible. James Cornelius, the curator of the Abraham Lincoln Collection at the Abraham Lincoln Presidential Library and Museum in Springfield, took a special interest in this project and was extremely helpful. I am grateful to him and his colleagues at the library.

The Sangamon Valley Collection at the Lincoln Library, Springfield's public library, was another important resource. Special thanks to Karen Graff, who not only helped me research 1850s Springfield but also introduced me to the horseshoe sandwich, a Springfield-created delicacy that consists of meat, toast, french fries, and a cheese sauce. It's delicious!

Susan Haake, curator at the Lincoln Home National Historic Site, was also encouraging and supportive. Lance Ingmire graciously shared stories of his great-great-uncle Frederick Ingmire, Fido's photographer. Forensic veterinarian Melinda Merck generously donated her time to examine the Fido photographs and render her professional analysis.

As usual, my literary agent, Jane Dystel of Dystel & Goderich Literary Management, was superb throughout this project. Thank you, Jane. Your encouragement means everything to me.

Same goes for my editor at Chicago Review Press, Jerry Pohlen, whose support never wavered, even when the manuscript came in a few words short and a few weeks late.

While most of my research was conducted in Springfield, much of this book was written in Ulaanbaatar, the capital of Mongolia, where my wife, Allyson, was posted as a US Foreign Service officer. She and our daughter, Zaya, were a constant source of inspiration. They are the lights of my life.

I would be remiss if I failed to confess that I am a cat person, not a dog person, and that my family's feline companions, Copernicus and Fraiti, were excellent company while I wrote this book. They didn't seem to take it personally that it was about a dog. Sadly, Miss Fraiti passed away at the ripe old age of eighteen, just days before the manuscript was completed. She is dearly missed.

Much about Abraham Lincoln's life is shrouded in myth, mystery, and controversy—even his pet dog. I hope the reader will forgive any lapses in rigorous historiography contained herein. I merely wanted to tell the story of an ordinary dog and his extraordinary master, living through turbulent times. Abraham Lincoln once loved a yellow mutt named Fido very much, and that mutt returned his master's affection in kind.

BIBLIOGRAPHY

Angle, Paul M. *"Here I Have Lived": A History of Lincoln's Springfield.*
  Chicago: Abraham Lincoln Book Shop, 1971.
Ashby, Williams. "He Shaved Abe Lincoln." *Afro-American* (Balti-
  more, MD), December 31, 1938.
Bayne, Julia Taft. *Tad Lincoln's Father.* Lincoln, NE: University of
  Nebraska Press, 2001.
Boas, Norman Francis. *Abraham Lincoln: Illustrated Biographical Dic-
  tionary: Family and Associates, 1809–1861.* Mystic, CT: Seaport
  Autographs Press, 2009.
Bonsper, Pam. "Lincoln's Dog Fido." *Coastal Canine,* Winter 2012.
Brown, Caroline Owsley. "Springfield Society Before the Civil War."
  Journal of the Illinois State Historical Society 15, nos. 1–2 (1934).
Browne, Francis F. *The Every-Day Life of Abraham Lincoln: A Biography
  of the Great American President from an Entirely New Standpoint,
  with Fresh and Invaluable Material.* New York: N. D. Thompson
  Publishing, 1886.
Burlingame, Michael. *Abraham Lincoln: A Life.* 2 vols. Baltimore:
  Johns Hopkins University Press, 2008.
Campbell, Bruce Alexander. *The Sangamon Saga: 200 Years; An Illus-
  trated Bicentennial History of Sangamon County.* Springfield, IL:
  Phillips Brothers, 1976.
Chase, Mary Ellen. *Victoria: A Pig in a Pram.* New York: W. W. Nor-
  ton, 1963.
Colver, Anne. "At Home with the Abraham Lincolns." *McCall's,*
  February 1957.
Cook, John C. "Reminiscences of Springfield." *Illinois State Journal*
  (Springfield, IL), February 20, 1927.

Cornelius, James. "Sniffing Around for Abraham Lincoln's Dog Fido." Abraham Lincoln Presidential Library and Museum blog. Accessed June 27, 2014. http://alplm.tumblr.com /post/80497508509/fido.

Donald, David Herbert. *Lincoln*. New York: Simon & Schuster, 1995.

Ehrmann, Max. "Lincoln's Visit to Terre Haute." *Indiana Magazine of History* 32, no. 1 (1936).

Finsen, Lawrence, and Susan Finsen. *The Animal Rights Movement in America: From Compassion to Respect.* New York: Twayne Publishers, 1994.

Gertz, Elmer. "The Black Laws of Illinois." *Journal of the Illinois State Historical Society* 56, no. 3 (Autumn 1963).

Goodheart, Adam. "Lincoln: A Beard Is Born." *New York Times* blog, November 24, 2010. http://opinionator.blogs.nytimes.com /2010/11/24/lincoln-a-beard-is-born/.

———. *1861: The Civil War Awakening.* New York: Albert A. Knopf, 2011.

Goodwin, Doris Kearns. *Team of Rivals: The Political Genius of Abraham Lincoln.* New York: Simon & Schuster, 2006.

Grier, Katherine C. *Pets in America: A History.* Chapel Hill, NC: University of North Carolina Press, 2006.

Grimm, David. *Citizen Canine: Our Evolving Relationship with Cats and Dogs.* New York: PublicAffairs, 2014.

Guither, Harold D. *Animal Rights: History and Scope of a Radical Social Movement.* Carbondale, IL: Southern Illinois University Press, 1998.

Hart, Richard E. *Springfield, Illinois' Nineteenth Century Photographers (1845–1900).* Springfield, IL: Self-published, 2005.

Henderson, Jenny. *The Top Hat: An Illustrated History of Its Styling and Manufacture.* Yellow Springs, OH: Wild Goose Press, 2000.

Henderson, Sandy. "The Glorification of Fido and Old Bob." *Illinois Times* (Springfield, IL), February 10–16, 1983.

Hickey, James T. "The Lincoln Account at the Corneau & Diller Drugstore, 1849–1861: A Springfield Tradition." *Journal of the Illinois State Historical Society* 77, no. 1 (Spring 1984).

Holzer, Harold. *Father Abraham: Lincoln and His Sons.* Honesdale, PA: Calkins Creek, 2011.

———. *Lincoln President-Elect: Abraham Lincoln and the Great Secession Winter 1860–1861.* New York: Simon & Schuster, 2008.

Hudak, Mike. "Abraham Lincoln: Vegetarian and Animal Rights Advocate?—A Review of the Evidence." *Broome County History Bulletin* 8, no. 2 (Fall 2009).

Illinois Humane Society. *Annual Report*, February 1911.

Illinois State Journal (Springfield, IL). "Fido Was Assassinated." February 20, 1893.

Illinois State Register (Springfield, IL). "Dogs Played Important Part in Lincoln's Life, History Shows." September 24, 1954.

———. "Hogs Had Run of the City in Middle 1800s." March 11, 1968.

Klockenkemper, James J. "Letter from Barber Friend to Lincoln Full of High Praise." *Spokane Daily Chronicle*, February 8, 1952.

Krupka, Francis O. *Historic Structure Report: Abraham Lincoln Home*. Springfield, IL: Lincoln Home National Historic Site, 1992.

Kunhardt, Dorothy Meserve. "Lincoln's Lost Dog." *Life*, February 15, 1954.

Kunhardt, Dorothy Meserve, and Philip B. Kunhardt Jr. *Twenty Days*. Secaucus, NJ: Castle Books, 1993.

Kunhardt, Philip B., Jr. "The Original Touchy-Feely: 'Pat the Bunny' Turns 50." *New York Times*, December 23, 1990.

Kunhardt, Philip B., III, Peter W. Kunhardt, and Peter W. Kunhardt Jr. *Looking for Lincoln: The Making of an American Icon*. New York: Albert A. Knopf, 2008.

Lawler, Edward, Jr. "The President's House in Philadelphia: The Rediscovery of a Lost Landmark." *Pennsylvania Magazine of History and Biography*, January 2002.

Lincoln, Abraham. "The Bear Hunt: An Original Ballad Never Before Printed." Edited by Charles T. White. *Atlantic*, February 1925.

Oates, Stephen B. *With Malice Toward None: A Life of Abraham Lincoln*. New York: HarperPerennial, 1994.

Penn State. "Domestication of Dogs May Explain Mammoth Kill Sites and Success of Early Modern Humans." *ScienceDaily*, May 29, 2014. www.sciencedaily.com/releases/2014/05/140529154155.htm.

Power, John Carroll. *History of the Early Settlers of Sangamon County, Illinois*. Springfield, IL: Edwin A. Wilson, 1876.

Pratt, Harry E. *Personal Finances of Abraham Lincoln*. Springfield, IL: Abraham Lincoln Association, 1943.

Randall, Ruth Painter. *Lincoln's Animal Friends: Incidents About Abraham Lincoln and Animals, Woven into an Intimate Story of His Life.* Boston: Little, Brown, 1958.

————. *Lincoln's Sons.* Boston: Little, Brown, 1955.

Rice, Charlie. "The Strange Fate of Lincoln's Dog." *This Week,* February 2, 1969.

Rowan, Roy, and Brooke Janis. *First Dogs: American Presidents and Their Best Friends.* Chapel Hill, NC: Algonquin Books of Chapel Hill, 2009.

Russo, Edward J. *Prairie of Promise: Springfield and Sangamon County.* Woodland Hills, CA: Windsor Publications, 1983.

Sandburg, Carl. *Abraham Lincoln: The Prairie Years and the War Years.* New York: Galahad Books, 1993.

Serpell, James, ed. *The Domestic Dog: Its Evolution, Behaviour and Interactions with People.* Cambridge, UK: Cambridge University Press, 1995.

Singer, Peter. *Animal Liberation.* New York: Avon Books, 1990.

Smith, Lenora Y. *The Legend of Fido 1861: Lincoln's Old Yaller Dog.* Springfield, IL: Self-published, 1964.

Strickland, Arvarh E. "The Illinois Background of Lincoln's Attitude Toward Slavery and the Negro." *Journal of the Illinois State Historical Society* 56, no. 3 (Autumn 1963).

Swanson, James L. *Bloody Times: The Funeral of Abraham Lincoln and the Manhunt for Jefferson Davis.* New York: HarperCollins, 2011.

Veblen, Thorstein. *The Theory of the Leisure Class.* New York: Dover Publications, 1994.

Walker-Meikle, Kathleen. *Medieval Pets.* Woodbridge, Suffolk, UK: Boydell Press, 2012.

White, Charles T., and Gilbert J. Greene. *Lincoln the Comforter: Together with a Story of Lincoln's First Pet, and a Narrative by Captain Gilbert J. Greene.* Hancock, NY: Herald Press, 1916.

Wisdom, Jennifer P., Goal Auzeen Saedi, and Carla A. Green. "Another Breed of 'Service' Animals: STARS Study Findings About Pet Ownership and Recovery from Serious Mental Illness." *American Journal of Orthopsychiatry* 79, no. 3 (July 2009).

INDEX